Otton
Cookery

TÜRÂBİ EFENDİ

DÖNENCE

DÖNENCE

OTTOMAN COOKERY
TÜRABİ EFENDİ

ISBN 975-7054-51-8

Editor

ALTAY İLTAN AKTÜRK

KEMAL ÖZDEMİR

Cover Designed by

FIRAT ÖZDEMİR

Photos
NADİR EDE, KADİR KIR, ASİTANE Ar□ivi
DÖNENCE DİABANK

Mise an Page

DÖNENCE BASIM VE YAYIN HİZMETLERİ

Printed in Turkey

DÖNENCE / GÜNAYDIN OFSET

3rd edition

Published by

DÖNENCE BASIM VE YAYIN HİZMETLERİ

Tayyareci Sami sokak no:18 kat : 2 - ISTANBUL

Tel: 0090 212 511 18 89 -0090 216 336 76 15

e-mail: donenceyay@hotmail.com

TURKISH COOKERY BOOK.
A COLLECTION OF RECEIPTS,

DEDICATED TO
THOSE ROYAL AND DISTINGUISHED PERSONAGES,
THE GUESTS OF HIS
HIGHNESS THE LATE VICEROY OF EGYPT,
ON THE OCCASION
OF THE BANQUET GIVEN AT WOOLWICH,
ON BOARD HIS HIGHNESS YACHT THE FAIZ-JEHAD,
THE 16TH JULY 1862.

COMPILED BY TURABI EFENDI,
FROM THE BEST TURKISH AUTHORITIES.

PREFACE

I have been induced, through the persuasion of numerous friends acquainted with the East, and who have a grateful recollection of its "savoury dishes," to translate the following Receipts, which I have taken the greatest pains to render accurate and concise.

During the visit of the late Viceroy of Egypt to England, he gave a banquet on board his yacht, at which some of England's fairest ladies and greatest statesmen were guests, and were unanimous in their approval of the Turkish cuisine.

Emboldened by this recollection I send my little book to the press, in the hope that may efforts to confer a benefit on the culinary art may not be entirely thrown away.

TURABI EFENDI
LONDON, August 1864

PUBLISHER'S FOREWORD

The first publication in a foreign language regarding Ottoman Cuisine was this book entitled, "A Turkish Cookery Book", written by Türabi Efendi and printed in the year 1864.

Türabi Efendi clearly indicated in the preface of the work that he prepared the cuisine recipes through the assistance of Turkish cuisine specialists.

The majority of the recipe in the book were acquired from Mehmet Kamil's Melceü't Tabbahin (Chef's Shelter), known as the first Turkish cookbook, which was printed in 1844.

While Turkish Cuisine essentially continues where Ottoman Cuisine leaves off, it is a synthesis of the cuisines of ali the nations that were once a part of the Ottoman State. In other words, Ottoman Cuisine is a rich cornucopia comprised of Balkan, Aegean, Caucasian, Syrian, Lebanese and Anatolian cuisines combined in a single kettle. The place where this cuisine was developed, applied and shown as its own cuisine is İstanbul.

While Ottoman cuisine is regarded as the richest in the world, it is made up of ali sorts of vegetables, natural grains, fruits, red meat, fish, game and poultry.

This new publication contains material not found in the original edition whereas translation errors were edited as well.

We wish to thank both Türabi Efendi, whose identity is not definitely known, but may have been an Ottoman Citizen who knew English, as well as the writer of Melceü't Tabbahin (Chef's Shelter), Mehmet Kamil, whose recipes were incorporated in this book, for bequeathing us with this remarkable work.

INDEX

KÖFTELER
MEATBALLS

KIZARTMALAR
FRIED DISHES

BÖREKLER
PASTRY, WITH MEAT

SOĞUK TATLILAR

COLD SWEET DISHES

KAYGANALAR

OMELETS

SALATALAR

SALADS

TURŞULAR

PICKLES

MEYVE TATLILARI

STEWED FRUITS

PART I.

Çorbalar / Soups

The soups in Turkey are almost the same as they are in Europe:
I therefore give the translations of the following fowl soups especially to Turkey. No. 1 and No. 2 are the recipes of the stock for those soups, to which particular attention should be paid, as they will
frequently be referred to in many of the dishes. The translation of
the names of the dishes into English will be found opposite the Turkish names in the Index.

Et Suyu

BROTH or STOCK for SOUPS

Ingredients

4 lb shin of beef or knuckle of veal
4 onions (cut in four crosswise)
1 stick celery
Salt
4 quarts water

NO.1

Wash the meat well, and put it in a stew pan with salt, onions, celery, and water. Then set the pan on the fire, when it starts boiling, skim it well, and let it simmer until the meat separated from the bones. Then pass the broth through a sieve and use it for the following soups.

Tavuk Suyu

FOWL BROTH or STOCK for SOUPS

Ingredients

2 Fowls
2 onions (cut in four crosswise)
1/2 stick of celery
Salt
4 quarts water

NO.2

Put in a stew pan the fowls, salt, onions, half a stick of celery, water and put it on the fire. As soon as boiling commences, skim it well, and let it simmer until the fowls are quite tender; then pass the broth through a sieve, and it is ready for use. The fowls may be served with rice prepared as Susuz Pilav (see p. 113).

Ekşili Çorba
SOUR SOUP

Ingredients

2 lb mutton (cut into pieces the size of small walnuts)
2 tbls flour
2 egg yolks
1 tbls vinegar or juice of a lemon
Salt
Pepper
2 pinches cinnamon
4 quarts water

Wash the meat and put it in a stew pan with salt, and water. Then put the pan on fire. When boiling, skim it well, and let it simmer until the pieces of meat are tender, and skim off the fat. Then put in a basin the flour and mix it with water to form a smooth thin batter and add it to the broth by degrees, stirring at the same time, so as to prevent it from getting lumpy. Let it simmer till the smell of flour is dispersed, and then take it off. Then beat up the egg yolks in a small saucepan with wine vinegar or lemon-juice, set it on a slow charcoal fire, and keep it stirring with a wooden spoon until a little thick. Then take it off, and add it gradually to the soup, stirring it quickly at the same time, to prevent the eggs from curdling.
Then pour it in a tureen, sprinkle a little pepper and cinnamon over, and serve.
This soup is generally made at public meetings, on occasion of a marriage e.t.c

Şehriyeli Çorba

VERMICELLI SOUP

Ingredients

4 pints of chicken broth
2 chicken hearts
2 chicken livers
6 ounces vermicelli
White pepper
2 pinches cinnamon
Salt

Put broth (No.2) in a stew pan with the hearts and the livers of chickens, half cooked and cut into small dice, and a little salt; put it on the fire. When boiling, add vermicelli, and let it boil until tender; then remove the pan, and pour the contents in a tureen, sprinkle a little white pepper and cinnamon over, and serve.

Erişte Çorbası

MACARONI SOUP

Macaroni soup is done exactly as above, only it takes two or three times longer than the vermicelli.

Nohut Çorbası

CHICK-PEA SOUP

Ingredients

1 cup chickpeas
6 cups broth
2 pinches cinnamon
Salt

Scald the chickpeas, and remove the pods, or skins; then put them again into the same water, and boil them until they become quite soft. Then drain and mash them with the back of a wooden spoon, and pass them through a sieve into a stew pan; then moisten it with broth (No.1 or No. 2) and set it on the fire. Let it simmer until to a nice consistency and then pour it in a tureen, sprinkle a little cinnamon over, and serve with toasted or fried bread in small dice.

Tarhana Çorbası

"TARHANA" SOUP/CURD SOUP

Ingredients

4 French roll slices (crumbled)
1 cup yoghurt (see p...)
5 cups broth

Put the French rolls in a stone mortar, with yoghurt and pound them well together, and let it remain for one night. Then put it in a stew pan, and moisten it by degrees with broth (No. 1) as is required by bruising and beating it up smooth with a wooden spoon. Then set it on a moderate fire, and let it simmer for about an hour. Take it off, pour it into a tureen, and serve it with bread cut into small dice and fried in fresh butter.

The addition of a small quantity of cream or milk will render it still more pleasant.

Terbiyeli Ciğer Çorbası
LIVER SOUP WİTH SAUCE

Ingredients

1 lamb's or sheep's light
3 pints of broth no.1
2 egg yolks
2 lemon or 1 tbls vinegar
2 pinches cinnamon
Salt
1 cup Water

Get a lamb's or sheep's light and cut it into small dices, put them in a stew pan with a little salt, and a small quantity of water; put it on the fire until the lights are nearly cooked, then add three or four pints of broth (No.1), and let it simmer till the pieces of lights are quite done.

Then beat up the egg yolks in a small saucepan, with the juice of one or two lemons, or with wine vinegar, and stir it on a slow fire with a wooden spoon till a little thick; then take it off and pour it gradually into the soup, stirring it quickly at the same time, to prevent the eggs from curdling.

Then pour the soup into a tureen, sprinkle a little cinnamon over, and serve.

Pirinç Çorbası
RICE SOUP WİTH SAUCE

Ingredients

1 cup rice
3 pints of broth
2 egg yolks
2 lemons
2 pinches cinnamon
Salt

Wash the rice and put in into a stew pan, with salt, and broth (No. 1 or No. 2); set the pan on the fire. Let it boil gently until the rice is soft and add the yolk of two eggs prepared as above with lemon juice, pour the soup into a tureen, sprinkle a little cinnamon over, and serve.

İşkembe Çorbası

TRIPE SOUP WITH SAUCE

Ingredients

3 pounds tribe
2 pints of water
2 pints of broth
3 egg yolks
3 lemons
Salt

Put bullock's tripe into a stew pan with water and salt and set it on the fire. When boiling, skim it well, and let it simmer until it loosens up; then take it off and skim off the fat. Take out the tripe, and chop it up very fine; put it again in the pan with what liquor is left, which you have previously passed through a sieve. Add broth (No.1), set it again on the fire, and let it simmer for ten minutes or so. Then add the egg yolks prepared as in Terbiyeli Ciğer Çorbası, and serve.

Although the sound of tripe is not enticing, yet it will be found to make an excellent soup.

Balık Çorbası
FISH SOUP

Ingredients

3 lb Grey mullet
6 tbls olive oil
6 onions (finely chopped)
1 pint of wine vinegar
2 pints of hot water
4 egg yolks
2 lemons
2 pinches of Saffron
1/2 bunch of Parsley
1/2 bunch of Mint
2 pinches cinnamon
Cayenne pepper
Salt

Get very fresh grey mullet, clean it well, and sprinkle a little salt over it; then put olive oil in a stew pan, with onions, and 1/2 ts salt. Put the pan on the fire till the onions are partly browned. Add a handful of washed parsley, and the same of mint, both chopped fine, and fry them a little together with the onions.

Then add the wine vinegar, and hot water, and boil it for twenty or thirty minutes. Then pass the liquor through a cloth or sieve into another stew pan, and place the fish in it; put it on the fire and let it simmer till the fish is done; then take it out and extract all the bones, cut the fish in pieces and put them into the tureen; then pass the liquor again through a cloth into a stew pan.

Then put in a basin the egg yolks, the juice of one or two lemons, and half a teacup of water previously coloured with saffron. Beat them up all together, add it gradually to the liquor and set it on a moderate fire for ten or fifteen minutes, stirring it all the time with a wooden spoon, without permitting it to boil. Then pour it over the fish, sprinkle a little cinnamon and a pinch of cayenne pepper over, and serve.

Turbots, soles and flounders may be done in the same way.

Kırma Tavuk Kebabı

PART II.

KEBAPLAR
KEBABS, OR ROAST MEATS

Şiş Kebabı

SKEWER KEBAB

Or PIECES OF MUTTON, or BEEF DONE, ON SKEWERS

Ingredients

5 lb mutton
4 onions
6 tomatoes or 4 tbls tomato paste
Salt
Pepper
3-4 pinches cinnamon

Get loin or leg of mutton and cut it into pieces of the size of an egg. Then chop the onions, and sprinkle them over the meat with salt, pepper, and cinnamon. Rub in well with hands, and let it remain covered for two or three hours; if in season, squeeze half a dozen tomatoes, and pass the juice through a sieve into a basin; if not, mix four or five tablespoonfuls of preserved tomato sauce in three quarters of a pint of water.

Then pass the pieces of meat one by one on the skewers, place them in front of the fire, and gradually turn them, as soon as the meat begins to brown, baste it now and then with the tomato juice. When nicely cooked, dish it up, and serve hot.

Tavuk Kebabı

ROAST CHICKEN

Ingredients

1 chicken
Salt
Pepper
2 pinches cinnamon
Flour

Clean the chicken, and sprinkle salt, pepper and cinnamon over, and let it remain for one or two hour. Then put it on the split, and place it before the fire.

When the gravy begins to drop, sprinkle a little flour over, and continue the same till the chicken is just upon being done; then wrap it up with some thin paper, and place it again before the fire for twenty minutes or so; then take the paper off, and serve hot.

Kuş Kebabı

BIRD KEBAB

Ingredients

2 lb mutton or lamb meat
1 teacup onion juice
1 tablespoon flour
Salt
Pepper
2 pinches cinnamon
Cumin

Cut mutton or lamb meat in pieces the size of walnuts. Then pour a small teacup of raw onion-juice over and mix with sufficient salt and pepper; rub it well, and let them remain for about two hours. Then pass them on the skewers one by one, place them in front of a moderate fire, and turn them continually. As soon as the meat begins to get brown, and the gravy drops, sprinkle a little flour over. When the meat is thoroughly done, sprinkle a little cinnamon and cumin over, and serve hot.

Kırma Tavuk Kebabı

CREASED ROAST CHICKEN

Ingredients

2 chickens
Salt
Pepper
3 pinches cinnamon
1/2 teacup onion juice
2 ounces butter (melted)

Clean the chickens, then split each one with a sharp knife, and remove the whole of the bones. Then cut the flesh in small pieces, but without separating one piece from another. Sprinkle them with salt, pepper, and cinnamon; then rub them in with raw onion-juice, and let them remain for an hour. Then pass them on skewers, and place them before a moderate fire; turn them continually, and when the chickens begin to brown, baste them with fresh butter with a quill, until they are nicely cooked. Dish up, and serve hot.

The juice of the onion is not at all offensive, but improves the flavour, and the smell disperses in cooking.

Süt Kebabı
KEBAB WITH MILK

Ingredients

2 lb mutton or lamb meat
2 cups milk
2 tbls flour
Salt
Pepper
2 pinches cinnamon

Cut mutton or lamb meat in pieces as the size of a small egg; sprinkle with your fingers salt, pepper, and cinnamon over, and let them remain for an hour or two, then place them in a stew pan, and cover them with milk. Set it on the fire until the milk begins to boil, and then take it off the fire, skim it well, and take the pieces of meat out.

When cold, pass them on skewers one by one, put them before a moderate fire, and turn them gently; at the same time, get ready some fresh milk, and keep it hot by the side of the fire. As soon as the meat commences to brown, baste it with a quill now and then with the hot milk. When the gravy drops freely, sprinkle a small quantity of flour over the meat.

Continue the same until it is nicely cooked. Then dish it up tastefully, sprinkle a little cinnamon over, and serve hot. This is a light and pleasant Kebab.

Muhzır Kebabı

BEADLE'S KEBAB

Ingredients

2 lb mutton meat
2 onions (chopped)
Salt
Pepper
2 pinches cinnamon
1 fat cloth

Cut the mutton meat in pieces the size of an egg. Then sprinkle onions, salt, pepper and cinnamon over and mix. Let them remain for one or two hours, then pass the pieces of meat on the skewers, and wrap them up with some thin fat cloth.

Place them before the fire, and turn them gently. As soon as the meat begins to brown, baste it with the gravy that drops from it. When done, dish it up tastefully, and serve hot.

Hacı Osman Kebabı

THE KEBAB OF PILGRIM OSMAN

Ingredients

2 lb mutton or lamb meat
2 onions (chopped)
Salt
Pepper
2 pinches cinnamon

Cut mutton or lamb in pieces the size of walnuts, and rinse them with water. Then sprinkle onions, salt, pepper, and cinnamon over and mix. Put them in a stew pan without any water, and cover it airtight.

Set it on a moderate charcoal fire for nearly four hours, and stir it now and then.

Be careful, for if the fire is too slow the meat will not brown nicely. When the pieces of meat are a nice colour and tender, dish them up, and serve hot.

Tavşan Kebabı

ROAST HARE

Ingredients

1 hare
5-6 cloves of garlic
1 teacup wine vinegar
1/4 lbs butter
Salt
Pepper

Procure a nice hare, clean it well, cut it into pieces, each about the size of a kidney; put them in cold water, and let them remain for two or three hours. Then take them out, and try them in a cloth, season with sufficient salt and pepper, and let them remain for twenty minutes or so.

Then pass them on the skewers one by one, put them before a moderate fire. While they are turning, pound the garlic cloves in a mortar with a little salt; add a small teacup of wine vinegar, stir it well, pour it in a small saucepan. Add fresh butter, place the saucepan on a moderate charcoal fire, and stir well with a wooden spoon until the butter is melted. Then take off, and keep it hot. As soon as the gravy begins to drop from the hare, baste it with the above mixture with a quill or a paste brush, and when you have basted it three or four times, remove the skewers from the fire, and beat the pieces of hare all over lengthways with a very thin cane.

Put the skewers again before the fire; beat them two or three times, as before. When nicely cooked, dish up tastefully; pour the remaining sauce from the basting over them.

Then place the dish covered, on a hot stove, or on a slow charcoal fire, until the sauce or gravy is nearly absorbed by the pieces of hare, and serve while hot.

Nevi Diğer *Tavşan Kebabı*

ROAST HARE II

Ingredients

1 hare
5 lb mutton meat
3 onions (chopped)
1 bunch of parsley (chopped fine)
1 tbls flour
1 fat cloth
Salt
Pepper

Cut a hare into pieces as above, and mix with as many pieces of loin of mutton as there are of hare, all of equal size.

Then sprinkle onions over, with a handful of parsley, salt and pepper. Rub the hare and mutton with these, and let them remain covered with a cloth for one or two hours. Then pass them on skewers; first mutton, then hare, and so on until the whole of them is on skewers. If handy, wrap them up with some thin fat cloth; put them before the fire, and turn them gently. As soon as the gravy begins to drop, sprinkle a little flour over. When the meat is nicely cooked, dish it up, pour the gravy over, and serve.

Kıymadan Fırın Kebabı

BAKED MINCE MEAT KEBAB

Ingredients

2 lb mutton
3 onions (chopped)
2 tbls butter
3 tbls pine nuts
3 tbls currants
Salt
Pepper
2 pinches cinnamon
1 fat cloth

Mince a leg of mutton or any other part of raw mutton 2 pounds of meat. Put onions in a stew pan with some fresh butter, and partly fry them. Add the minced mutton with pine nuts, currants, salt, pepper, and cinnamon. Stir round with a spoon until the minced meat is also partly fried. Then cut a fat cloth in pieces about the size of vine leaves, divide the minced meat in each piece, and wrap it up to the shape of a small cup, or any shape yon may fancy. Lay them on a baking tin, place it in a hot oven until nicely browned, dish up tastefully, and serve.

Tas Kebabı

PIECES OF MUTTON IN BASIN

Ingredients

2 lb mutton
2 onions (chopped fine)
1 1/2 pint of broth
3/4 lb rice
Salt
Pepper
2 pinches cinnamon
Chilli Pepper
Thyme

Cut leg or loin of mutton in pieces the size of small walnuts, wash them with cold water, and dry them in a cloth. Then sprinkle onions over, with salt, pepper, and other spices, rub them well in the meat, and let it remain covered for about two hours. Put the pieces of meat in a convenient basin, and place it upside downwards in the centre of a clean baking-tin an inch and a half deep, and the bottom of which must be strong enough to bear the heat of the fire.

Then place a tureen on a charcoal fire, and over which set the baking-tin for about an hour and a half. When the gravy has run out and is absorbed, pour in the baking-tin broth. No. 1. Alternatively, No. 2, and add well-washed rice and spread it even around the basin. When the broth is absorbed, and the rice is still hard, sprinkle some more broth over. Each grain should be soft, and well separated. When done, take the baking-tin off the fire, and, just at the time it is wanted, remove the basin from the centre of it, and serve as it is, with a napkin pinned round the baking-tin.

This is a celebrated and an exquisite dish, and it is pleasing to the eye. In Turkey the baking-tins are made of copper, and the insides are plated; they are circular, and from one or two feet in diameter.

Ciğer Kebabı
LIVER KEBAB

Ingredients

1 lamb's liver
1 fat cloth
2 cloves garlic
1/2 teacup wine vinegar
1 cup broth
Salt
Pepper

Cut, as much as you want, sheep or lamb's liver in dice, an inch and a half square and pass them on skewers. Wrap each one with a thin piece of fat cloth, place them before a moderate fire, and turn them slowly until the liver is nicely roasted. When done, dish it up. Then pound garlic in a mortar very well and add wine vinegar, broth, a little salt and pepper, stir it well with a wooden spoon. Pour it over the liver, put the cover on.

Place it in the oven, or on a charcoal fire covered for five minutes or so, and then serve.

Doldurulmu Kuzu Kebabı
STUFFED LAMB

Ingredients

1 lamb
3/4 lb butter
4 onions (chopped)
Onion juice (from 4-5 onions)
6 tbls pine nuts
6 tbls currants
3 lbs rice
Salt
Pepper
2 pinches cinnamon
Water

Get the whole of a small lamb with the liver and the heart, place it in a large saucepan or iron pot without the liver and the heart, cover it with water, set it on the fire and let it boil for ten or fifteen minutes. Then chop up the liver very fine together with the heart, put butter in a stew pan with onions, put it on the fire, and let them stew till nearly brown. Add the liver and the heart, with pine nuts, and currants. Stir until the liver begins to cook, and then add well-washed rice, salt, pepper, and cinnamon. Keep stirring, and add now and then a little of the liquor in which the lamb is boiled, until the rice is rather soft.

Then stuff the lamb all over with rice, rub some onion-juice over and place it in a baking- tin, and bake it a nice brown on both sides in a very hot oven. When done, dish up, and serve.

This is the most famous way of cooking a lamb in Turkey. It can also be stuffed before boiling it, and roasted instead of baked.

Biryan -Orman Kebabı

FOREST KEBAB

Ingredients

1 lamb
Onion juice (from 4-5 onions)
Salt
Pepper
2 pinches cinnamon

Get a whole or a lamb, already cleaned; rub it all over with onion-juice, sufficient salt and pepper. Pass it on a pole sufficiently long, and wrap the sheep up in sheets of paper. Then make a large wood or charcoal fire, thrust in the ground at each end of the fire, half a yard distant, a stake, with fangs sufficiently large and strong for the pole to rest on with the sheep.

Then place the pole on them, and keep turning it gently. Put a dripping-pan under the sheep to catch the gravy, and baste the sheep with a bunch of feathers, or a piece of clean linen tied at the top of a stick.

When half done remove the papers and turn it quickly. When nicely browned all over, take out the pole, dish it up, sprinkle some cinnamon over, and serve.

Somon Balığı Kebabı
ROASTED SALMON

Ingredients

2 lb salmon
2 lemons
1 bunch of parsley
Bay leaf
Salt
Pepper

Get the salmon in one piece, remove the bones, and cut it in pieces the size of an egg. Sprinkle sufficient salt and pepper over, with a handful or two of parsley chopped fine, and let them remain for about an hour. Then pass them on skewers with a bay leaf between each piece; put them before a moderate fire, and turn them until the fish is nice browned. Dish it up tastefully, with some parsley and one two lemons cut in quarters round it, and serve hot.

Turbot, swordfish, codfish, halibut, or sturgeon, may be cooked in the same way.

Uskumru Balığı Kebabı
ROASTED MACKEREL

Ingredients

2 lb mackerel
1 bunch of parsley
1/2 bunch of fennel
2 lemons
Bay leaf
Salt
Pepper

Get fresh mackerel and cut off the point of the head. If large, divide each one in three pieces; if small, in two pieces. Wash and dry them in a cloths sprinkle them with sufficient salt and pepper, and a handful or two of chopped parsley mixed with fennel, and let them remain for an hour. Then put them on skewers, with a bay leaf between each piece, and cook them as above.

Eels and grey mullets may be done in the same way.

PART III.

KÜLBASTILAR BROILED MEATS &C., IN VARIOUS WAYS

İstiridye Külbastısı / Broiled Oysters

Tavuk Külbastısı

BROILED CHICKEN

Ingredients

1 chicken
1 cup broth no. 2
Salt
Pepper
4 pinches cinnamon

Split a cleaned chicken lengthways and remove the whole of the bones with a sharp knife. Cut the flesh in four or five pieces as you fancy, and beat the thicker parts even with a rolling pin.

Sprinkle them with sufficient salt and pepper, and a little cinnamon, and let them remain for one or two hours. Then place them on a gridiron, set it on a moderate charcoal fire, and constantly turn them with a pair of tongs. When nicely browned, lay them in a stew pan, and cover them with broth (No. 1. or No. 2); put the pan on a moderate charcoal fire, and let simmer until tender. Dish up, and serve hot.

Koyun ve Kuzu Külbastısı

BROILED MUTTON OR LAMB

Ingredients

1 mutton neck
Salt
Pepper
1/2 ts sweet marjoram
1 bunch of parsley
1 onion (chopped fine)

Cut from the neck of mutton or lamb as many cutlets as are required, remove the bone at the thick end, and beat them out with a rolling pin or a small chopper.

Sprinkle with your fingers sufficient salt and pepper, and a small quantity of sweet marjoram. Rub them well in the chops and place them on a gridiron. Set it on a moderate charcoal fire; turn them frequently with a pair of tongs. When nicely cooked, serve whilst hot. If a handful or two of parsley together with an onion place over the cutlets, it will make an improvement.

Tencere Külbastısı

BEEF OR VEAL BROILED, AND THEN FINISHED IN A STEW PAN

Ingredients

2 lb veal meat
Salt
Pepper
3-4 cloves of garlic
1/2 teacup wine vinegar
1 cup broth

Cut as much as is wanted of rump steak or veal in slices the size of a hand, and about half an inch thick. Sprinkle a little salt and pepper over, place them on a gridiron. Set it on a moderate charcoal fire, and frequently turn them as above. When nicely browned, place them in a stew pan with a few cloves of garlic peeled, and wine vinegar and broth (No. 1.) put the pan with the cover over on a moderate charcoal fire, and let it simmer until tender, and serve.

If garlic is not fancied, place over the meat one or two onions, sliced fine and fried in fresh butter, but without the vinegar.

Haşlama Balık Külbastısı

FISH SCALDED AND THEN BROILED

Ingredients

2 lb grey mullet
1 teacup olive oil
1/2 bunch of parsley
1/2 teacup wine vinegar
1 cup broth
Salt
Pepper

Get some grey mullet, or any other fish you fancy, clean it well, and then scald it. Rub a gridiron with a little olive oil, and place the fish over. Set it on a moderate charcoal fire, and turn it now and then until both sides are nearly browned.

Take it off, then lay one or two handfuls of chopped parsley on the bottom of a baking dish or tin, and lay the fish over with a little salt and pepper. Add half a teacup of wine vinegar, and two of broth

(No. 1).

Put it on a charcoal fire until the broth is absorbed, then dish it up, and serve hot.

Scalding the fish before broiling renders it pleasant.

Somon Balığı Külbastısı

BROILED SALMON

Ingredients

1 salmon
Salt
Bay leaf
1/2 bunch of parsley
2 onions
2 lemons

Cut from the tail end of a small salmon as many thin slices as are wanted, and rub them with a little salt. Then cover a gridiron with some bay leaves, lay the slices of fish over, set it on a moderate charcoal fire, and turn the fish often. When nicely browned on both sides, take it off, then cover the bottom of a dish with some finely chopped parsley and onions, place the fish over, with one or two lemons cut in quarters round the dish, and serve hot.

Morina Balığı Külbastısı

BROILED CODFISH

Ingredients

1 codfish
2 tbls flour
1/2 teacup olive oil
1/2 bunch of parsley
2 onions
2 lemons
Salt

Cut from a small codfish as many slices as are required, rub them with a little salt, and dip them in flour. Then rub a gridiron with olive oil, lay the fish over, set it on a moderate charcoal fire, and turn the fish often. When nicely browned on both sides, take it off, then cover the bottom of a dish with some finely chopped parsley and onions, place the fish over, with one or two lemons cut in quarters round the dish, and serve hot.

Uskumru Balığı Külbastısı
BROILED MACKEREL

Ingredients

4 mackerels
2 tbls olive oil
1/2 bunch of parsley
1 onion
1 lemon
Salt

Cut off the points of the heads of the fish and sprinkle them with sufficient salt, and let them remain for about an hour.

Then rub a gridiron with some olive oil, lay the mackerel over, and broil gently on a charcoal fire.

When done, dish it up, place some chopped parsley mixed with finely sliced onions over, and serve hot. A lemon squeezed over the fish will improve the flavour.

İstiridye Külbastısı
BROILED OYSTERS

Ingredients

2 lb oysters
Salt
Pepper
1 tbls olive oil
1 lemon (sliced)

Open the oysters as are wanted, lay them on a gridiron, sprinkle with your fingers a little salt and pepper over each one, with a few drops of olive oil. And set the gridiron on a charcoal fire.

When the oysters are nicely broiled and begin to stick to the shells, dish them up in their shells, and serve with lemon.
Scallops are broiled in the same way, only with a pinch or two of finely chopped fennel in each one.

PART IV.

YAHNİLER - PİLAKİLER
FRICASEED OR STEWED MEATS

Uskumru Balığı Yahnisi / Stewed Mackerel

Beyaz Yahni

WHITE STEW

Ingredients

2 lb mutton meat
1 1/2 cups chickpeas
3 onions (sliced)
4 cups water
4 slices of bread
Salt
Pepper

Cut of a leg or any other part of mutton in pieces the size of walnuts or eggs, wash and place them in a stew pan with a little salt and pepper. Cover them with water and put it on a charcoal fire. Let it boil for about twenty minutes, skim it well, then add chickpeas previously scalded in water and onions. Let it simmer until it forms a nice thick gravy at the bottom of the pan and the meat and peas are tender. Then dish it up with two or three slices of toasted bread on the bottom of the dish, and serve while hot.

Kırmızı Yahni

RED STEW

Ingredients

2 lb lamb or mutton meat
1 1/2 cups chickpeas
3 onions (sliced)
3 tbls butter
4 slices of bread
Salt
Pepper

Cut as much as is required of a leg of lamb or mutton in pieces, and boil as above. Then add finely sliced onions, fried in fresh butter, and chickpeas previously scalded in water; cook and serve as White Stew.

Dana EtindenPapaz Yahnisi

PRIEST'S STEW (STEWED VEAL)

Ingredients

5 lb veal meat
4 onions (sliced)
5 heads of garlic
1 teacup vinegar
Salt
Pepper
Cumin

Cut loin of veal in pieces the size of eggs; place them without any water in rather deep stew pan, with onions, garlic, salt, pepper, a little cumin, and a teacup of wine vinegar.

Put the cover over the pan air tight, or paste it round with paper, so that no steam shall escape. Put it in an oven, or simmer it on a moderate fire for about three or four hours. When done, dish it up tastefully, and serve. Be particular in pasting round the cover, and the fire must not be fierce, or the meat may burn.

Kızartma

A KIND OF FRIED MEAT

Ingredients

2 lb mutton leg or sirloin
1 cup yoghurt
1/2 lb butter
2 onions (sliced thin)
Salt

Cut mutton in pieces the size of large eggs, place them in a saucepan with sufficient salt, and cover them with water. Set it on the fire, and let it boil for twenty or thirty minutes. Skim it well, then take out the pieces of meat, and rub them all over with yoghurt.

Then fry them a nice brown in fresh butter, and place them in a saucepan with onions, fried a nice brown in fresh butter. Add the liquor in which the pieces of mutton were boiled, put the cover over the pan, set it on a moderate charcoal fire until it forms a nice thick gravy at the bottom, and the meat is tender. Then dish it up, and serve.

This dish is generally made at public meetings on occasion of a marriage, e.t.c.

Maydanozlu Yahni

STEWED MUTTON WITH PARSLEY AND SAUCE

Ingredients

2 lb mutton
1 onion (sliced thin)
1 bunch parsley
3 tbls butter
3 eggs
2 lemons
4 cups water

Cut mutton in pieces the size of small kidneys, boil and skim it as above, then add a few onions sliced thin and partly fried in fresh butter, and let it simmer until the meat is nearly cooked. Add two or three handfuls of picked parsley, and let it simmer for ten or fifteen minutes longer then beat up the egg yolks in a basin with the juice of lemons. Pour it into a small saucepan, set it on a slow fire, and stir it with a wooden spoon till it begins to thicken, without permitting it to boil. Then dish the stew up tastefully, pour this sauce over, and serve.

Sarımsaklı Yahni

ANOTHER KIND OF STEWED MUTTON FLAVOURED WITH GARLIC

Ingredients

2 lb mutton
6 heads of garlic
2 onions (sliced thin)
1 bunch of parsley
3 tbls butter
3 eggs
2 lemons
1 1/2 teacup wine vinegar
3 teacup water
Salt
Pepper - Cumin

Cut some mutton into pieces the size of walnuts, peel the garlic, and mix salt, pepper, and cumin. Then lay seven or eight cloves of garlic on the bottom of a stew pan, sprinkle a pinch of the seasoning, and add some pieces of mutton. Season again, then garlic, then mutton, and so forth, until the whole is laid.

Then add onions, fried in fresh butter, a teacup and a half of wine vinegar, and water, set it on a charcoal fire. Let it simmer until the meat is nicely browned and tender, dish up, and serve.

Kuzu Kızartması

FRİCASSEED LAMB, WİTH RICE

Ingredients

1 lamb's leg
1 lamb's liver
1 lamb's heart
2 lb yoghurt
6 tbls butter
4 onions (sliced)
3 tbls pine nuts
2 tbls currants
2 pint chicken broth
1 lb rice
Salt
Pepper
2 pinches cinnamon
Cumin
3 pinches allspice

Cut lamb meat in pieces the size of kidneys, then dip each piece in yoghurt and fry them a nice brown in fresh butter.

Place them in a stew pan with onions fried in butter, salt and pepper; cover them with hot or cold water. Set it on a charcoal fire, and let it simmer gently until it forms a nice thick gravy at the bottom of the stew pan. While the meat is cooking, chop up the liver and the heart of a lamb together, and then fry it in fresh butter with a little salt. When nicely done, add a handful of pine nuts skinned, and currants, and a little mixed spice; stir it with a wooden spoon for five minutes or so; then place it in a saucepan, with some of the gravy of the lamb, and two pints of broth (No. 2); set it on a charcoal fire with the cover over. When boiling, add well washed rice, stir it, put the cover over, and let it boil until each grain is rather soft, but separate.

Then take it off, wrap round the lid a wet cloth, to prevent the steam from escaping, and put it by the side of the fire for twenty minutes or so; each grain will then swell up and be well separated, and no moisture be left. Then dish it up in the form of a dome, arrange the pieces of lamb over tastefully, and serve hot.

This is an excellent dish, and the pilaff, or the rice, gives it a pleasing appearance.

Tavşan Yahnisi

STEWED HARE

Ingredients

1 hare
5 onions (sliced thin)
1 1/2 wine vinegar
8 cloves garlic
4 tbls butter
Salt
Pepper

Cut a hare in pieces about the size of kidneys, wash them well, and let them remain for one or two hours, or until thoroughly cleaned from blood. Then place them in a stew pan with onions, salt and pepper. Cover them with water, set it on a charcoal fire until the hare is half cooked.

Then strain the liquor into o basin, and take out the onions. Put the liquor in a stew pan with vinegar, and garlic. Set it on the fire, and let it boil until the liquor is reduced to half. Then fry the onions in fresh butter, and put them over the hare with the liquor. Put it on the fire, and let it simmer until a nice thick gravy is formed at the bottom; then dish it up, and serve.

Although the hare is stewed in various ways, this is considered one of the best.

Domatesli Kızartma Yahni

STEWED MUTTON, WITH TOMATO

Ingredients

4 lb mutton meat
6 tbls butter
4 onions (sliced)
10 green tomatoes (cut in four)
3 lb tomatoes (ripe)
Salt
Pepper

Cut five or six pounds of the best part of mutton into pieces about the size of kidneys, wash and dry them in a cloth. Then fry them a nice colour in fresh butter, place them in a stew pan with onions fried in fresh butter, tomatoes, salt and pepper. Then squeeze ripe tomatoes in a basin, pass the juice through a cloth or sieve, and then pour it in the stew pan with sufficient water to cover the meat.Set it on a charcoal fire with the cover over, and let it simmer until the liquor is reduced to a nice thick gravy; then dish it up tastefully, and serve.

Sığır Eti Yahnisi
STEWED BEEF

Ingredients

6 lb rump steak
15 cloves of garlic
3/4 lb butter
3 lb potatoes (sliced)
2 lb tomatoes
Salt
Pepper

Cut rump-steak into rather long slices, half or three-quarters of an inch thick, then tie them together one over the other with a piece of string, as if one piece of meat.

Then with the point of a knife, make about fifteen holes here and there, and stick in each o clove of garlic peeled. Place it in a stew pan with fresh butter, set it on a moderate charcoal fire with the cover over for about three hours, turning the meat every half hour. Then add potatoes partly fried in butter, and the juice of ripe tomatoes with a little water, and sufficient salt and pepper. Put the cover over the pan and let it simmer until the meat and the potatoes are well done; then cut the string off the meat, dish up tastefully, and serve.

Sığır Eti Yahnisi II
STEWED BEEF WITH MACARONI

Ingredients

6 lb beef
2 glass vinegar
10 pepper-corns
1 orange peel
15 cloves of garlic

Get in one piece leg or rump of beef, cover it with vinegar, and let it remain four and twenty hours. Then wash it, and make deep holes all over, fill the holes with pepper-corns, orange-peel, and cloves of garlic peeled. Place it in a stew pan with three-quarters of a pound of fresh butter, set it on

3/4 lb butter
3 lb tomatoes
3 pint of water
Salt
Pepper
2 1/2 lb macaroni

a moderate charcoal fire for three or four hours, turning it now and then. When nicely browned, add the juice of tomatoes with water, and sufficient salt and pepper, ant let it simmer until the meat is nicely cooked. Then take it out, and keep it hot; put in the stew pan about two pounds and a half of the best macaroni: if the liquor is not enough, add some of the broth (No. 1), and boil till the macaroni is tender; let it be rather firm to the touch. Dish it up, sprinkle some finely grated cheese over, then place the beef in the centre of the macaroni, and serve.

Tavuk Yahnisi
STEWED FOWL

Ingredients

1 fowl or chicken
2 lb mutton neck
4 lb butter
8 onions (sliced)
1 1/2 cups chick peas
3 tbls wine vinegar
Salt
Pepper

Cut a well-cleaned fowl in two lengthways, place it in a stew pan with the middle of a neck of mutton, and cover them with water. Put in a little salt, set it on the fire, and let it boil until the fowl is half cooked, and skim it well. Then take the fowl out and fry it a nice colour in fresh butter, then place it in a stew pan with onions fried in butter, previously boiled a little soft and skinned chick-peas, wine vinegar, and the liquor in which the fowl is boiled. Add sufficient salt and pepper, put it on a slow charcoal fire, and let it simmer until it forms a nice thick gravy at the bottom of the pan, and the peas are tender. Then dish it up tastefully, and serve.

The mutton can be served with parsley and butter over as a dish, if approved of.

Güveç Balığı / Fish Baked in an Earthen Pan

Güveçte Balık

FISH BAKED IN AN EARTHEN PAN

Ingredients

1 fish
5 onions (sliced)
1 teacup olive oil
1/2 bunch of parsley (chopped)
1/2 tea cup wine vinegar
1 tea cup water
4 tomatoes (cut in four crossways)
Salt

Get any fish you fancy, scale and clean it well. If a large one, cut it in three or four pieces, sprinkle some salt over, and let them remain for a little while. Then put olive oil in a frying-pan with onions, and a handful or two of chopped parsley. Put it on the fire and stew it rather brown. Then lay half of it on the bottom of a rather deep baking-dish, and place the fish over. Then place the other half of the onions and parsley on the top, with the oil that is left in the frying pan and add half a teacup of wine vinegar, one of water, and tomatoes. If the tomato is not in season, one or two table spoonfuls of preserved tomato sauce will do instead. Put it in the oven for twenty minutes or so. When nicely baked, dish it up, and serve.

All kinds of fish may be done in the same way.

Uskumru Balığından Papaz Yahnisi

PRIEST'S STEWED MACKEREL

Ingredients

6 mackerel
4 onions (sliced)
1/2 cup olive oil
1/2 bunch of parsley
1/2 bunch of fennel
1/2 tea cup wine vinegar
2 tea cup fish broth
Salt
Pepper
2 pinches cinnamon

Take out the inside of half a dozen mackerel, and wash them. Then boil them in water for one or two minutes; when cold, remove the bones. Then fry the onions partly brown in olive oil. Lay the half on the bottom of a stew pan, with a handful of picked parsley mixed with a little fennel, and pour in what oil is left in the frying pan. Then place the pieces of mackerel over, and the other half of the onions, with the same quantity of parsley and fennel on the top. Add wine vinegar, fish broth, salt and pepper. Then put the pan on a moderate charcoal fire with the lid on, and let it simmer gently until the fish is nicely done. This will take about fifteen or twenty minutes, dish it up, sprinkle a little cinnamon over, and serve.

The addition of one or two tomatoes cut in four makes an improvement in the above: if not in season, a tablespoon of preserved tomato sauce will do instead.

Papaz Yahnisi II
PRIEST'S STEWED FISH

Ingredients

2 lb fish
4 onions (sliced thin)
1/2 bunch of parsley (chopped fine)
2 tbls tomato sauce
1/2 teacup wine vinegar
1/2 teacup olive oil
1 teacup water
Salt / Pepper

Get any fish you fancy, and clean it well. Then mix onions with parsley and lay the half on the bottom of a stew pan. Then place the fish over and the other half of the onions and parsley on the top. Add salt and pepper, tomato sauce, wine vinegar, olive oil, and water. Set the pan on a charcoal fire, and let it simmer gently until the fish is cooked, dish it up, and serve.

Kılıç Balığı Yahnisi
STEWED SWORDFISH

Ingredients

5 lbs swordfish
3 tbls flour
1 egg (beaten)
1 bunch of parsley (chopped fine)
1 cup olive oil
12 cloves of garlic
3 pinches Cayenne pepper
2 lemons
2 teacup water
Salt

Procure swordfish in one piece cut it in slices, wash them, and sprinkle a little salt over. Then dip them in flour, and then in egg, and partly fry them in olive oil. Then spread one handful of parsley on the bottom of a stew pan with five or six cloves of garlic, lay the slices of fish over, and spread the same quantity of parsley and garlic on the top. Then add sufficient salt, Cayenne pepper, the juice of lemons, and water. Put the pan over a charcoal fire with the lid on, and let it simmer gently for twenty minutes, or until the liquor is nearly absorbed; dish it up, and serve. Salmon and sturgeon may be done in the same way.

Yağsız Balık Yahnisi / Stewed Fish without Oil

Yağsız Balık Yahnisi
STEWED FISH WITHOUT OIL

Ingredients

8 red mullets
3 pints of water
4 onions (cut in four crossways)
2 onions (chopped fine)
3 heads of garlic (only the outer skin peeled)
1 bunch of parsley (chopped fine)
1/2 lemon
Salt
Pepper

Get the red mullets, take out the insides, well clean them, and sprinkle some salt over. Then put water in a saucepan, with for onions cut in four crossways, and garlic. Put it on the fire, and let boil until the water is reduced to about one pint. Then take the onions and the garlic out, throw the onions away, but squeeze the garlic, and add the pulp to the liquor. Then mix fine chopped onions with parsley, sprinkle a little salt and pepper over, and well rub them. Then stuff the fish with it and lay it carefully in a stew pan, pour the liquor over, set it on a charcoal fire, let it simmer until the fish is nicely cooked. Then dish it up, squeeze lemon over, and serve hot. Mackerel may be done in the same way.

Kefal Balığı Pilakisi
STEWED GREY MULLETS

Ingredients

6 grey mullets
1 tbls butter
1/2 teacup olive oil
3/4 lbs onions (sliced)
1/2 bunch of parsley (chopped)
2 lemons
Salt
2 pinches cayenne pepper

Take out the gills and the insides of very fresh grey mullets, and cut them in two crossways. Wash and sprinkle them with a little salt, and let them remain for an hour. Then put in a stew pan fresh butter, olive oil, a little salt, and onions.

Put it on the fire and let the onions stew, but not brown. Then lay the fish over, cover it with water, and let simmer for twenty or thirty minutes.

When nearly done, add parsley, cayenne pepper, and the juice of lemons, and let it simmer for four or five minutes longer, then dish it up, and serve hot.

Yağsız Uskumru Pilakisi
STEWED MACKEREL, WITHOUT OIL

Ingredients

8 mackerel
1 bunch of parsley (picked)
2 pinches mastic (powdered)
1 pint of water
1 lemon

Take out the insides and the gills of seven or eight mackerel, wash them, and cut off the points of the heads and the tails. Then lay some on the bottom of a stew pan, place half of the fish over.

Then sprinkle a little powdered mastic over, some parsley again; then lay the other half of the fish over, mastic again, then parsley. Add water and put the pan on a charcoal fire, and let simmer gently for twenty minutes or so; dish it up, squeeze a lemon over, and serve.

Tekir Balığı Pilakisi

STEWED RED MULLETS

Ingredients

8 red mullet
3 onions
3 eggs
2 lemons
1/4 pint olive oil
1 bunch of parsley (chopped)
1/2 pint of water
2 pinches cinnamon
2 pinches allspice
Salt
Pepper

Take out the gills and the insides of seven or eight red mullets, and wash them. Then peel the onions, and well pound them in a mortar. Add a little allspice, cinnamon, salt, pepper, the juice of lemons, the egg yolks, and a little water, and beat them up well together with a wooden spoon. Then pour it over the mullets, and let them remain for about two hours. Put an olive oil in a flat stew pan, with a plate of parsley; put it on the fire, and just scald it. Then add water, and a teaspoon salt. When boiled, lay the mullets in with the ingredients, and let it simmer for fifteen or twenty minutes, dish up tastefully, and serve hot.

İstiridye Pilakisi

STEWED OYSTERS, WITH EGG SAUCE

Ingredients

2 lb oysters
4 tbls olive oil
1/2 bunch of parsley (chopped)
2 teacups water
3 egg yolks
1 lemon

Open as many oysters as are wanted, take them out of the shells, and put them in a basin. Put olive oil in a saucepan, set it on the fire. When hot, place parsley and the oysters over; add one or two cups of water, and let it boil for ten minutes or so. Then beat up the egg yolks in a saucepan, with three or four tablespoon the liquor of the oysters and the juice of a lemon; put it on a slow fire, and keep stirring with a wooden spoon until the egg begins to thicken. Then dish the oysters up, and pour this sauce over, and serve.

Dana Eti Pilakisi
STEWED VEAL

Ingredients

2 lb veal neck or loin
1 bunch of parsley (picked)
1 lemon
Salt
Water

Cut as much as wanted of a neck or loin of veal in pieces the size of kidneys; wash and place them in a stew pan, with a little salt, and cover them with water; set it on the fire. When boiling, skim and simmer until the meat is nearly cooked, then add a handful or two of picked parsley, and let it simmer for a few minutes longer.

Two minutes before taking it off the fire, add the juice of one lemon; dish it up, and serve.

PART V.

KÖFTELER / MEATBALLS

Kebab Köfte / Fried Meatball

Kebab Köfte
FRIED MEATBALL

Ingredients

3 lb mutton leg
1/2 bunch of parsley
3 onions (peeled)
1 crumb bread
5 tbls butter
1 lemon
1/2 tbls flour
Salt
Pepper
2 pinches cinnamon

Put on a chopping board either a raw leg of mutton, or beef, or veal, half a handful of parsley, onions peeled, and the crumb of a French penny roll, sprinkle a little salt, pepper, and cinnamon over, and mince them very fine together until like a paste. Then make it up in shapes of small buns, or any shape you may fancy, and fry them a nice colour in fresh butter. Then put in basin flour, the juice of a lemon, and a little salt and set it on a slow fire. Keep stirring until it is a nice consistency. Then dish the meat up tastefully, and pour the gravy over, and serve hot. Alternatively, serve it with finely sliced onions and chopped parsley over, instead of gravy, if approved of.

Susuz Köfte
MEATBALL WITHOUT BROTH

Ingredients

2 lb mutton meat
1 juice of an onion
1/2 teacup water
1/4 lbs butter
Salt
Pepper
2 pinches cinnamon

Mince very fine as much as is required of the best part of raw mutton, sprinkle a little salt, pepper, and cinnamon over; then knead well with onion juice, and make it into balls the size of walnuts. Then put in a bowl or basin water, and fresh butter; arrange the balls of meat in the bowl, and place it into an iron pot, put the cover over and paste it round, or wrap a wet cloth round it, to prevent the steam from escaping. Set it on a moderate fire, and let it simmer for about two hours; dish it up tastefully, and serve hot.

Maydanozlu Köfte
MEATBALL WITH PARSLEY

Ingredients

2 lb mutton
5 tbls butter
3 onions (sliced thin)
1 bunch of parsley (chopped)
3 teacup broth
3 tbls wine vinegar
Salt
Pepper

Mince very fine a sufficient quantity of raw mutton with a little salt and pepper; then make it into balls the size of nectarines, and fry them a nice brown in fresh butter, then partly fry in the same butter onions, and add parsley, and keep stirring for two or three minutes. Then lay them on the bottom of a saucepan, and place the balls of meat over. Add broth (No.1) and wine vinegar. Set it on a slow charcoal fire, and let it simmer for twenty minutes or so, and serve.

Terbiyeli Köfte
MEATBALL WİTH EGG-SAUCE

Ingredients

2 lb mutton
5 tbls butter
3 onions (peeled)
1 bunch of parsley (chopped)
3 teacup broth
3 tbls wine vinegar
3 eggs
2 lemons
Salt
Pepper
Water

Mince the best part of raw mutton, with two or three onions peeled, and a little salt and pepper. Then make it in balls the size of nuts, put them in a saucepan half full of water, set it on the fire until done. Then beat up the egg yolks, with the juice of a lemon or two and a little salt. Pour it in a saucepan, put it on a slow fire, and keep stirring until it begins to thicken. Then add three or four tablespoons (one at a time) of the liquor in which the meatballs have been boiling. Stir it for two or three minutes longer, then dish the meat up, pour this sauce over, and serve hot.

Kimyonlu Köfte
MEATBALL WITH CUMIN

Ingredients

1 lb mutton or beef
2 onions (peeled)
1 onion (sliced thin)
1 bunch of parsley
Salt
Pepper
Cumin
5 tbls butter

Mince very fine as much as wanted of either raw mutton or beef, with onions; sprinkle sufficient salt, pepper, and cumin. Then knead well and make it up in the shape of small buns, and fry them in fresh butter, or broil them on a grill until nicely brown.

When done, arrange them in a dish, and serve hot, with chopped parsley mixed with thinly sliced onions round the dish.

Maydanozlu Sıkma Köfte
MEATBALL SQUEEZE WITH PARSLEY II

Ingredients

2 lbs mutton
4 onions (peeled)
2 tbls rice flour
1 bunch of parsley (chopped fine)
2 lemons
Salt
Pepper
Cumin
5 tbls butter
1 1/2 teacup broth

Mince very fine as much as is wanted of a raw leg of mutton. Then pound onions in a mortar, and squeeze the juice over the meat. Then knead it well with a handful of rice flour, salt and pepper, and make it into balls the size of small peaches. Then roll them in parsley until they are well covered and arrange them in a saucepan. Add the juice of lemons, with a teacup of broth (No. 1.) and set it on a moderate charcoal fire with the cover over. When the liquor is nearly absorbed, add some more broth, and let it simmer until nicely cooked. Dish it up tastefully, and serve hot. This is a light and exquisite dish.

Mücmer

FRIED MEATBALL WITH EGG

Ingredients

3 lb mutton or veal meat
3/4 lb butter
1/2 teacup water
3 onions (chopped fine)
1/2 bunch of parsley (picked)
1 slice of bread (crumbled)
3 eggs
Salt
Pepper

Mince either raw mutton or veal, place it in a stew pan with 2 ounces of fresh butter, water, a little salt, and set it on the fire. When boiling, stir round with o wooden spoon until nicely browned and the moisture is dispersed. Then take it off, and put the meat in a basin, add onions, parsley, the crumb of a French roll previously soaked in water, eggs, and a little salt and pepper, and mix them well together. Then put a sufficient quantity of fresh butter in a convenient frying pan, place it on a charcoal fire.

When boiling, pour in the preparation. When set and one side is nicely browned, turn the other side, when nicely browned, dish up, and serve quite hot.

Mücmer II

FRIED MEATBALL WITH EGG II

Ingredients

2 lb mutton or beef
3 onions
Pilaff (see p....)
3 eggs
1 bunch of parsley (chopped fine)
Salt
Pepper
5 tbls butter

Mince a raw beef or mutton together with onions; then pound it well in a mortar with an equal quantity of Ordinary Pilaff (see p.111) break over it the eggs, sprinkle sufficient salt and pepper with a handful of parsley. Then knead well all together, and let it remain covered for half an hour; then divide it in the egg size pieces, and fry them in boiling fresh butter. When all are nicely browned, dish up tastefully, and serve hot.

Mücmer / Fried Meatball with Egg

Fasulye Mücmeri
FRIED MINCED MEAT WITH FRESH BEANS

Ingredients

1 lb French beans
1/2 lb butter
1 tbls flour
4 eggs
5 tbls fried minced meat
Salt
Pepper

Scald the French beans with a little salt; when partly tender, put them on a board, and chop them up. Then place them in a basin, sprinkle some flour over, and rub them smooth with your hands; then add the eggs, fried meat, a little salt and pepper, and beat them up well with a fork. Put some fresh butter into the frying pan, set it on the fire until hot; and then fry one tablespoon of the mixture at a time. When all are fried a nice colour, dish them up tastefully, and serve hot.

Kadınbudu

LADY'S THIGH

Ingredients

2 lb mutton leg
3 onions (chopped)
1 cup rice (well washed)
4 eggs
1/2 lb butter
Salt
Pepper

Mince very fine the meat; add onions, rice, salt and pepper. Then knead well, and make it into shapes, as the fleshy part of a leg of capon. Then throw them in boiling water. When nearly cooked, take them out, and let them remain until cold. Then beat up the eggs, dip the pieces of meat in it, and fry them in hot fresh butter until nicely golden browned. When done, take them out, and let them drain. Dish up tastefully and serve hot.

Patlıcan Mücmeri

FRIED MINCED MEAT WITH EGG-PLANT

Ingredients

8 egg-plants
4 onions (chopped fine)
4 tbls fried minced meat
1 bunch of parsley (chopped fine)
3 eggs (boated up)
2 tbls butter
Salt

Cut the egg-plants in two lengthwise, take out the insides, and boil them a little in water with a little salt. Then take them out, and put them in a basin, add onions, previously fried in fresh butter, fried meat (prepared of raw mutton), parsley, salt, pepper, and eggs, and mix them well together.

Then butter a baking-pan, in which you will arrange half of the egg-plants, and stuff them with the above mixture; cover them with the remaining half, and bake them in a rather hot oven. When the egg-plants are shrunk and soft, they are cooked. Dish up, and serve.

PART VI.

TAVALAR / FRIED DISHES

Patlıcan Tava / Fried Eggplant and vegetable-marrow

Et Tavası

FRIED MUTTON

Ingredients

1 leg of mutton
2 onions (chopped fine)
1/2 lb butter
Salt
Pepper
2 pinches cinnamon

Cut the mutton into pieces the size of large eggs, split each piece in two or three places, and beat them out with a rolling-pin, sprinkle them with sufficient salt and pepper, cinnamon, onions, and let them remain for half an hour or so. Then put some nice butter in the frying pan, place it on the fire.

When quite hot, lay the pieces of mutton in it, and when nicely browned on one side turn them over, and do the same for the other side; then take them out, drain the fat, and serve.

Patlıcan Tavası

FRIED EGGPLANT

Ingredients

6 egg-plants
3 tbls flour
1/2 lb butter
Salt

Cut the eggplants in slices about half an inch thick, sprinkle them with salt, and let them remain about an hour. When the bitter juice is drawn from them, put the flour into a basin; mix it with water to form a thin smooth batter.

Then dip the eggplants in it, and fry them in fresh butter till a nice colour, turning them over. When done, take them out with a slice, let them drain, dish up, and serve.

Ciğer Tavası

FRIED LIVER WITH PARSLEY

Ingredients

1 lamb's or sheep's liver
4 tbls flour
1/2 lb butter
1 bunch of parsley (chopped)
2 onions (sliced thin)
Salt

Get a liver, wash, and cut it into large dice, sprinkle a little salt over; then dip them in flour, and fry them a nice brown in hot butter. When done, take them out and let them drain. Dish up, sprinkle parsley mixed with onions over, and serve very hot.

Kalkan Balığı Tavası

FRIED TURBOT

Ingredients

1 turbot
5 lemons
3/4 pint salted water
1/2 ounces saffron
1 cup olive oil or 1/2 lb butter
Salt

Get a turbot as large as is required, cut the flux off, wash and sprinkle it with sufficient salt.

Then cut lemons in slices and lay half of them on the bottom of a convenient dish, place the fish over, and cover it with the other half of the lemons.

Then pour the on it salted water coloured with half an ounce of saffron; place a plate or dish over, to press the fish slightly, and let it remain for one night.

The next day fry it a nice brown either in oil or fresh butter, and serve.

İzmarit Balığı Tavası
FRIED SMELTS

Ingredients

2 lb smelts
1 cup flour
2 eggs (beaten)
1 cup olive oil
1 lemon
Salt

Take out the insides of t smelts, wash and sprinkle them with a little salt; then dip them in flour, and then in egg. Fry them a nice colour in hot olive oil. When done, dish up tastefully, squeeze a lemon over, and serve hot.

Uskumru Balığı Tavası
FRIED MACKEREL

Ingredients

2 lb mackerel
2 onions (peeled)
2 lemons
3 eggs
1 cup olive oil
Salt
Pepper
2 pinches cinnamon
2 pinches allspice
2 pinches cumin

Take out the insides and the gills of mac-kerels, wash well, sprinkle them with a little salt, and let them remain twenty minutes or so. Then pound onions in a mortar, and add sufficient salt and pepper, all spice,cinnamon, cumin, the juice of two or three lemons, egg yolks and beat them well up. Then pour it into a pie-dish, roll the mackerel in it, and let them remain for about two hours; then fry them a nice brown in hot olive oil, turning them over.

When done, take them out with a slice and let them drain well, dish them up tastefully, squeeze a lemon over, if approved of, and serve hot.

Midye Tavası / Fried Mussels wiith Egg

Midye Tavası

FRIED MUSSELS WITH EGG

Ingredients

2 lb mussels
1 cup flour
2 eggs (beaten)
1 cup olive oil or
1/2 lb butter
1 lemon
Salt
Pepper

Open as many mussels as are required, and remove them from the shells, then dip them in flour, and then in eggs, fry them a nice colour in hot olive oil or fresh butter, dish up, sprinkle a little salt and pepper over, and serve hot with lemon.

PART VII.

Börekler / Meat Pastry

Tatar Böreği / Tartar's Pie

Yufka Böreği

MINCED-MEAT PIE

Ingredients

4 cups of flour
Salt
Pepper
Water
3 eggs
1 teacup broth
1/2 lb butter
AND
1 lb minced meat
2 onions (chopped fine)
OR
1 lb Cheese (grated)
1 bunch of fennel (chopped fine)
2 eggs

Place flour on the table-dresser or in a pan, make a hole in the centre, put in a little salt, and water, and stir it well up with the hands until it forms a nice paste. Then divide it into small pieces (say eight or ten), and roll them out thin, about the thickness of a sixpence, and the size of a baking-tin [1] intended for laying them in.

Then bake them soft, one by one, on a hot stove (such as crumpets are baked on), or a baking-sheet [2], which is placed over a tureen on a wood or charcoal fire. When done nicely on both sides, beat up the eggs in a basin, with a teacup of broth (No.1 or No. 2).

Then grease the baking-tin with fresh butter, and lay in half the pieces of paste one over the other, sprinkling some of the beaten-up egg; and fresh butter between each one with a quill or a paste-brush. Then lay some fried minced meat all over, half an inch thick, which is prepared from raw mutton or beef, and then cover it with the remaining pieces of paste, as above, egg and butter over again and place it in the oven until nicely browned on both sides.

When done, cut it like diamonds and serve. If finely chopped onions, stewed brown in fresh butter, is added to the fried minced meat, it will freshen it, and improve the flavour of it.

Cheese may be used instead of minced meat if preferred, thus: Grate some nice cheese, and then add to it the fennel, raw eggs, and a little pepper and salt. Mix them well together, and lay it between the pastes as above.

1) In Turkey the baking-tins are made of copper from two to three inches deep. They are circular, and from one to two feet in diameter.
2) The baking-sheets are made of iron. They are circular and slightly domed, and only used for baking layers of paste.

Yufka Böreği II

MINCED-MEAT PIE II

Ingredients

4 cups of flour
1/2 lb butter
2 lb minced meat
4 onions (chopped fine)
Salt
Water

Put the flour upon a pastry slab, make a hole in the centre, in which put a little salt, 3 ounces melted fresh butter, mix all together, then add sufficient water, and make it a softly paste. While working it, dip your hands in butter now and then, and knead it till a nice paste is formed. Then throw some flour lightly over and under, roll it out with a rolling pin to the thickness of half-a-crown. Put a tablespoonful of fried minced meat on it, mixed with finely-chopped onions stewed brown in fresh butter, or grated cheese, as above, about an inch and a half distance from each other. Wet lightly round them with a paste-brush, and place a similar piece of paste over all. Press round the part where the minced meat or cheese is, to make the paste stick; then cut them out like half an egg, and fry them in hot butter. When nicely browned, take them out, and let them drain, dish up in pyramid, and serve hot.
The addition of one or two raw eggs to the paste, while working it, will make an improvement.

Su Böreği
WATER PIE

Ingredients

4 cups of flour
3 eggs
3/4 lbs butter
Salt
Water
Minced meat or grated cheese

Put on the dresser, or in a basin the flour, with a little salt, mix it up with eggs and form it a flexible paste. Then cut it in twelve or fourteen pieces, and roll them out the size of the baking-tin intended for laying them in (see Minced-meat pie, p.71).

Then fill a saucepan or iron pot with water, put in sufficient salt, and set it on the fire. When boiling, scald the pieces of paste one by one, except two. When done, drain them, then dry them with a piece of clean cloth, and spread out the wrinkled parts carefully. Then put some fresh butter in a saucepan, and set it on the fire. When the butter is at proper heat, take it off, and, when rather cold, butter the baking-tin with it, in which lay one of the two unsalted pieces of paste, sprinkle a table-spoon of the butter over, on which lay half of the scalded pieces, sprinkling between each one spoonful of butter.

Then lay either minced meat or cheese (prepared as Minced-meat pie) all over, half an inch thick, cover it with the remaining pieces of paste that are scalded, sprinkling some butter between each one as before, and over which lay the other unsalted piece, well butter the top, and place it in a hot oven. When nicely browned, cut it in any shape you choose, dish up, and serve hot.

This is a noted pastry in Turkey, and it will be found light and agreeable.

Su Böreği / Water Pie

Süt Böreği
MILK PIE

Ingredients

3 pints of milk
5 eggs
6 tbls flour
1 salt
3 tbls butter

Pour milk in a basin; add the eggs, flour, and salt.

Beat up well together; then well butter a convenient baking-tin, pour in the preparation, and bake it a nice brown. When done, cut it in diamonds, and serve.

Tavuk Böreği
MINCED CHICKEN PIE

Ingredients

1 chicken
2 onions (chopped)
3 tbls butter
20 sheets of pastry (see Minced Meat Pie p. 71)
Salt
Pepper

Put a well-cleaned chicken in a saucepan with some water and a little salt, set it on the fire, and boil it until sufficiently tender and then take it out. When cold, remove the meat from the bones, and chop it up fine. Then stew one or two finely chopped onions in fresh butter until quite brown, and mix them well with the fowl. Add a little salt and pepper. then butter a baking-tin, in which place ten very fine layers of paste one over the other, sprinkling a little butter between each one. Then lay the minced fowl all over, and cover it with the same number of pastes as before, cut it in four crossways, pour a little hot fresh butter over, put it in the oven, bake it a nice brown, and serve hot.

Kol Böreği
ARM PIE

Ingredients

20 sheets of pastry (see Minced Meat Pie p. 71)
3 eggs
3 tbls broth
3/4 lb butter
Minced meat or grated cheese

Lay on the paste-board separately 20 sheets of pastry. Then beat up eggs in a basin, with broth (No. 1 or No. 2), dip a paste brush in it, rub it all over each piece of the paste, and fold them separately in two; then lay on each one lengthways any preparation you fancy, fold the two side edges over, and then the ends, thus making it an oblong shape. Make the others in the same shape, and fry them a nice brown on both sides in hot fresh butter. When all done let them drain, then dish up on a white napkin, and serve hot.

Kapak Böreği

COVER PIE or PIE COOKED IN A MOULD

Ingredients

20 sheets of pastry
3 onions
(chopped fine)
3 tbls butter
2 tbls almonds
2 tbls pine nuts
1 lb minced meat
Salt
Pepper
3 pinches cinnamon

Roll out as thin as a wafer twenty pieces of paste prepared with fresh butter and eggs. Then well butter the inside of a shallow and dome-like mould, in which lay carefully ten of the pastes one over the other, which must reach up the brim of the mould. Then place in a rather deep frying pan some finely minced raw lamb or mutton, onions, a little salt and a little fresh butter. Set it on the fire, and stew them partly brown. Then add skinned almonds skinned pine nuts, a little pepper and cinnamon; mix them well together with a wooden spoon. Then fill up the mould with this mixture, cover the top with the remaining ten pieces of paste. Then butter the bottom of a baking-tin, in which place the mould upside down. Put it in a hot oven, and bake it a nice brown. When done, turn it out of the mould on to a dish, and serve.

Türk Böreği

TURKISH PIE

Ingredients

1 1/2 lb flour
1/2 lb butter (melted)
2 eggs
1 ts salt
Water

Put on the dresser a pound of flour, make a hole in the centre, in which put a teaspoon of salt, break in the eggs, and mix. Then add sufficient water, and form it a flexible paste, divide it in two, and roll them out to the size of the baking-tin you intend to use. Then sprinkle some melted fresh butter over, and fold over the edges of the paste so as to hidethe butter, throw a little flour both under and over, and roll them out again as before, repeat the same five or six times more. Then butter the baking-tin, in which lay one of the two pieces of paste; then lay any preparation you choose all over it, half an inch thick, and cover it with the other paste. Then make about fifteen deep holes in the paste here and there with the point of a knife, and bake it a nice brown on both sides. When done, cut it in diamonds, dish up tastefully, and serve hot.

Sac Böreği

PIE COOKED ON A SHEET-IRON

Ingredients

1 lb flour
1/4 lb melted butter
2 lb minced meat
1onion (chopped very fine)
Salt
Pepper
4 pinches cinnamon
Water

Put in a basin the flour, and a little salt, mix it with sufficient water into a softly paste with your hands. Dry it off a little with flour until you have well cleared the paste from the basin, and let it remain for two or three minutes.

Then cut it into ten or twelve pieces, and roll them round with a rolling-pin the size of a dinner-plate, and as thin as a wafer. Then lay some finely-minced raw beef or mutton, mixed with onions, a little salt, pepper, and cinnamon over one half of each piece, half a quarter of an inch thick, and double the other half over. Press two edges with your fingers to make the paste stick. Then put a tureen on a charcoal fire, over which place a slightly-domed sheet-iron, the under side of which is previously cemented with ashes, to prevent it from getting fiercely hot. When moderately hot, dip a paste-brush in fresh butter and rub it all over.

Then place the pieces of paste over, and bake them a nice brown on both sides, now and then buttering them on both sides with the paste-brush.

When done, take them off with a slice, dish them up one over the other, and serve hot.

Paça Böreği

SHEEPS' TROTTERS PIE

Ingredients

1/2 calf's head or four calf's feet
10 sheet pastry (see Water pie p.75)
1 lb butter (melted)
Salt
Water

Get the head, or the feet of the calf, wash, and put them in a stew pan with sufficient water and salt. Set it on the fire, and let it boil until tender.

Then remove the meat from the bones, and cut it in small dice. Then prepare 10 sheets of pastry, but instead of scalding them in water, scald them in boiling fresh butter.

When all done, take out and place them in a colander, and, when free from fat, lay half of them in a rather deep and circular baking-tin one over the other, sprinkling between each piece some of the liquor in which the calf's head is boiled.

Then lay the pieces of calf's head all over, cover them with the remaining pieces of paste the same way as before, and bake it a nice colour; dish up, and serve.

İnce Börek

THIN PIE

Ingredients

1 1/2 lb flour
1/2 lb Mushrooms (chopped)
2 onions (chopped)
4 eggs
1 ts salt
1/2 lb butter (melted)
1/2 lb wheat-starch
Water
Minced mutton

Put the flour on a slab; make a hole in the centre and put salt and the eggs. Mix them all together, then add sufficient water, and form it a flexible paste. Then dip your hands into melted fresh butter, and work it for a few minutes longer.

Then divide it into thirty pieces the size of walnuts, sprinkle a little wheat-starch both under and over them, and roll them out one by one with a rolling-pin as thin as a wafer, or thinner than that if you can, and the size of the baking-tin you intend to lay them in. Butter the baking-tin, in which lay five of the pieces of paste one over the other, sprinkle a little fresh butter all over, and lay five more pieces over, butter again, and over which lay five more pieces, butter again.

Lay all over either minced mutton, mixed with mushrooms and onions, and previously stewed a nice brown in fresh butter, together with the meat, or cheese, as described in (see Minced-meat pie, p. 71), or any other ingredients you may fancy, and cover it with the remaining pieces of paste in the same way as before.

Then cut it in four crosswise, pour a little hot fresh butter over, and bake it a nice brown in a moderate oven. When done, dish up and serve.

Soğan Böreği
ONION PIE

Ingredients

6 onions (chopped)
3 tbls butter
3 eggs
Thin pie pastry (see p. 79)
Mushroom (if you fancy)
Salt
Water

Put in a saucepan chopped onions, a little salt, and some water, set it on the fire, and boil it for a few minutes. Then drain the onions, and put them in a frying pan with some fresh butter. Set the pan on the fire, and stew the onions until the moisture is dispersed, then beat up the eggs, and add it by degrees to the onions.

Put it on the fire again, and stir it for three minutes or so with a wooden spoon. Then take it off, and lay it between pieces of pastry and bake it a nice colour in moderate oven. The addition of a small quantity of mushrooms, chopped fine, and previously stewed with the onions in fresh butter, will make an improvement.

Fincan Böreği
CUP PIE

Ingredients

Thin pie pastry
Any of the pie ingredients
1 lb butter

Place on a paste-board three or four layers of thin pie pastry, one over the other. Then put ever in small lots any of the ingredients used in the preceding pastry, about an inch and a half distance from each other, wet slightly round them with a paste-brush, and cover them with the same number of pastes as before, but a little larger; then press over each lot with a Turkish coffee-cup, or a mould the size of an egg-cup, and cut them out, which will then be in the shape of the above cup. When all done, either fry them in hot butter, or arrange them in a baking-tin, previously buttered; sprinkle a little butter over them with a paste-brush, and bake them a nice colour in a moderate oven. When done, dish them up on a white napkin, and serve hot.

Tatar Böreği
TARTAR'S PIE

Ingredients

Thin pie pastry (seep.79)
1 lb Minced meat
2 tbls butter
Water

Roll out as many pieces as are wanted of thin pie pastry to the thickness of a sixpence. Then cut them in checks or square pieces, about two inches long and two broad.

Lay half a teaspoon of fried minced mutton or beef on one corner of each piece, and fold the other half over, thus forming it of a triangular shape. Press the two edges with your fingers to make the paste stick.

When the whole is ready, put on the fire a saucepan nearly full of water. When boiling, throw in the pieces of paste, and let them boil until nicely cooked, then drain them, and dish them up; sprinkle a little scalded butter over, with some nice Ayran (ayran is diluted yoghurt and water with salt), and a pinch of pepper, and serve hot.

Be careful that the pieces of paste do not stick to each other when boiling.

Tatar Böreği II
TARTAR'S PIE II

Ingredients

Thin pie pastry (see p.79)
1 lb minced meat
2 tbls butter
1/8 bunch of chervil
1/8 bunch of parsley
Water

Proceed exactly as Tartar's Pie. Then put on each piece half a teaspoon of minced beef, mixed with a little parsley and chervil, previously stewed with the beef in fresh butter, and double it as above.

When the whole is prepared, put on the fire a saucepan nearly full of water. As soon as it boils, throw in the pieces of paste, and let them boil till nicely cooked.

When done, drain them, and dish them up; sprinkle some hot butter over, and some nice cheese, grated fine, and serve hot.

PART VIII.

Bastilar - Sebzeler
Dishes Made with Meat and Vegetables

Bamya Bastısı / Mutton Stewed with Okras

Kabak Bastısı

MUTTON STEWED WITH VEGETABLE-MARROW

Ingredients

2 lb mutton
4 onions (sliced)
4 tbls butter
4 vegetable marrow
2 lemons
1 bunch mint (chopped)
Pepper
2 pinches cinnamon

Cut mutton or lamb meat in pieces about the size of walnuts; put them in a stew pan with a little salt, and cover them with water; set it on a charcoal fire.

When beginning to scum, skim it well, and let it simmer till the meat is nearly tender. Then put onions in a frying pan with butter, and fry them partly brown. Then peel the vegetable marrows, cut each one in four crossways, take out the insides, if seeded, and slice them three-quarters of an inch thick.

Lay some of the pieces of meat on the bottom of the stew pan and add some slices of vegetable marrow, with part of the fried onions, then meat, then pieces of vegetable marrow and onions, then meat, etc., until the whole of them are laid.

Then add the liquor in which the pieces of mutton were boiled and sufficient salt. If the liquor is not enough, add some of the broth (No. 1).

Set the stew pan on the fire, and let it simmer until the vegetable marrow is tender; then add the juice of one or two lemons, with a little mint; let it simmer for two minutes longer, and then take it off, dish it up, sprinkle a little pepper or cinnamon over, and serve hot.

Kabak Bastısı II

MUTTON STEWED WITH VEGETABLE-MARROW II

Ingredients

4 lb mutton loin
6 onions (sliced fine)
5 vegetable marrows
2 lemons
1 tbls sugar
4 cloves of garlic (pounded)
2 tbls mint (chopped)
Salt
Pepper

Get mutton loin, remove the bones, and cut the meat in pieces the size of walnuts. Then add six or seven onions sliced fine; sprinkle sufficient salt and pepper over, mix them all together, and rub them well with your hands. Peel vegetable marrow, and cut them in slices, as above; take out the insides, if seeded. Lay the bones of the mutton on the bottom of a convenient stew pan.

Then some slices of vegetable marrow over, then some pieces of mutton, then vegetable marrow, and so forth, until you have laid the whole. Cover them with water; add the juice of the lemons and a little salt.

Set it on the fire and let it simmers gently until the meat and the vegetable marrows are tender. Then add sugar, garlic, and two or three tablespoons of chopped mint.

Let it simmer for five or six minutes longer, then dish it up, and serve.

Bamya Bastısı

MUTTON STEWED WITH OKRAS

Ingredients

1 lb mutton
2 lb okra
3 onions (sliced)
3 tbls butter
2 lemons
Salt - Pepper
2 pinches cinnamon

Cut mutton into pieces about the size of walnuts, wash and place them in a saucepan, with sufficient salt. Cover them with water, and set the pan on the fire. When boiling, skim and simmer till the meat is half done. Fry the onions partly brown in fresh butter. Peel the stalk parts, and cut off the ends of okras. Then place the pieces of meat and the okras, together with the onions in layers as above. Add the liquor in which the meat was boiled, if not enough; add some of broth (No. 1) and a little salt. Put the cover over the pan, and set it on a charcoal fire until the meat and the okras are tender, and a nice gravy is formed at the bottom, which you will perceive by holding the pan on one side.

Just five minutes before removing it from the fire, add the juice of one or two lemons; and when done, dish up, sprinkle a little pepper and cinnamon over, and serve.

Bamya Bastısı II

MUTTON STEWED WITH OKRAS II

Ingredients

2 lb lamb meat
2 lb okras
3 onions (sliced)
2 lemons
3 cups broth
3 tbls butter
1/2 teacup water
Salt
2 pinches cinnamon

Cut one or two pounds of lamb in pieces, as above; place them in a stew pan with butter, salt, water and put on the fire. When boiling, stir round with a wooden spoon for about twelve minutes, or until it forms a whitish thick gravy at the bottom.

Lay the pieces of meat on the bottom of a rather deep and circular baking pan, and over which lay young okras, together with sliced onions, fried partly brown in fresh butter. Add the gravy, with the juice of one or two lemons, three cups of both mutton or beef broth, and a little salt, and bake it in a very hot oven until the okras are quite soft and nicely brown. Turn it gently on to a dish, without spoiling the shape, sprinkle a little cinnamon over, and serve.

Şeyh-ül Muşi

THE SHEIK'S or CHIEF'S ROAST

Ingredients

6 eggplants
3 ounces butter
1 lb mutton
3 onions (chopped)
3 tbls parsley (chopped fine)
3 tbls mint (chopped fine)
2 cups broth

Cut in four crosswise, without separating from the stalk, the eggplants. Then cut the inside part of each one, and throw it away, and put the eggplants in brine. Put in a frying pan fresh butter, minced raw mutton, onions, and fry them a nice brown.

Add parsley, and mint, sufficient salt and pepper, and mix them well together. Then stuff the eggplants with this, and tie them up separately with the stalks of parsley. Cover the bottom of a stew pan with some peeled parsley roots, in which lay the stuffed eggplants, and cover them with the broth (No. 1).

Set the pan on the fire with the cover over. When boiling, let it simmer until a nice thick gravy is formed at the bottom; then dish them up tastefully one over the other, and serve. Alternatively, dress them with some yoghurt, flavoured with a little garlic, if approved of, and then serve.

Medkune

MUTTON STEWED WITH EGGPLANTS

Ingredients

5 eggplants
2 lb mutton
2 onions (chopped)
2 lemons
6 cups broth no.1
Salt
2 pinches cinnamon

Peel the eggplants, cut them in slices about three-quarters of an inch thick, and partly scald them in salt water; then cut the mutton in pieces the size of walnuts, sprinkle onions over with a little salt, and rub them well together with your hands. Place into a stew pan the pieces of meat and the eggplants, in layers, cover them with broth, add the juice of lemons; put the pan on the fire with the lid on, and let it simmer until it forms a nice gravy at the bottom. Then dish it up, sprinkle a little cinnamon over, and serve. Artichokes may be cooked in the same way.

Marmarina

SPINACH WITH PASTRY

Ingredients

2 lb spinach
1/2 lb butter (melted)
4 sheets of pastry (see Minced Meat Pie, p.71)
4 eggs
1/2 lbs cheese

Well clean the spinaches, pick off the stalks, boil it for one or two minutes, let it drain, and chop it up very fine. Then well butter a rather deep and circular baking-tin, in which lay four or five very thin round pieces of puff-paste, one over the other; sprinkle a little fresh butter over with a paste-brush, and lay the spinach all over. Break into a basin the eggs, to which add half a pound of grated cheese, beat up well together, and lay it over the spinach. Put it in a rather hot oven, and bake it a nice colour. When done, cut it in four crosswise, and serve hot.

Yoğurtlu Şalgam

FRIED TURNIPS DRESSED WITH YOGHURT

Ingredients

4 turnips
1/2 pint of broth No.1
3 tbls butter
Salt
Yoghurt
Pepper

Peel the turnips, cut them in slices about or a half an inch thick; then boil them in water with a little salt, partly tender, and let them drain. When free from water, dip them in a baking-pan or a pie-dish that will bear fire; pour half a pint of broth (No. 1), over the turnips. Set the pan on a moderate charcoal fire, and let it simmers for eight or ten minutes. Then take it off, and lay some yoghurt over the turnips, over which sprinkle a little hot fresh butter, and a pinch of pepper, and serve hot.

Patlıcan Paçası

FRIED EGGPLANTS WITH SAUCE

Ingredients

- *4 eggplants*
- *1 cups of flour*
- *3 tbls butter*
- *4 cloves garlic*
- *1 teacup wine vinegar*

Cut the eggplants in slices a quarter of an inch thick, and put them in salt water for about ten minutes. Then dip them in flour, fry them a nice brown in fresh butter, and arrange them in a baking-dish. Then well pound the garlic cloves in a mortar, add a little salt, and wine vinegar. Pour it over the eggplants; place the dish on a moderate charcoal fire until the liquor is absorbed, then take it off, and serve.

Güveç Bastısı

MUTTON STEWED WITH A VARIETY OF VEGETABLES

Ingredients

- *4 lb mutton loin*
- *2 eggplants*
- *6 ounces French beans*
- *1/2 lb okras*
- *2 vegetable marrow*
- *4 green tomatoes*
- *4 onions (peeled)*
- *2 lemons*
- *1 1/2 tomato juice*
- *1/4 lb butter (optional)*
- *Salt*
- *Pepper*
- *3-4 pinches cinnamon*

Cut the mutton loin in pieces the size of walnuts. Wash and place them in an earthen stew pan, of which the lid must closely fit. Then cut the eggplants in four crosswise, and cut them in slices an inch thick. Sprinkle some salt over, and when the bitter juice is drawn from them, lay them over the meat. Add trimmed French beans, okras, the stalks and the ends cut off and stringed, one or two vegetable marrow, peeled and cut in slices as the eggplants green tomatoes cut in four crosswise, onions cut as the tomatoes, sufficient salt and pepper, the juice of lemons, and the juice of a pound and a half of tomatoes.

If the meat is not sufficiently fat, add a quarter of a pound of fresh butter, melted; put the lid over the pan, and cement round the edges with flour paste, so as to prevent the steam from escaping. Put it in a moderately hot oven for about three hours. When done, shake the pan gently, that the gravy may mix with the vegetables, and form a nice, thick sauce, then dish up, sprinkle a little cinnamon over, and serve.

Kuru Silkme

MUTTON FRICASSEED WITH EGGPLANTS

Ingredients

3 lb mutton meat
Salt
Pepper
3 tbls butter
3 eggplants

Cut mutton into small pieces as above, wash and dry them in a cloth, then place them in a stew pan with sufficient salt and pepper, set it on the fire, and stir with a wooden spoon until it begins to hiss, which indicates that all the moisture is dispersed. Then add butter, and keep stirring till the meat is nicely browned. When done, take them out with a hand-strainer, and place them in a dish and keep it hot. Cut eggplants in thin slices, sprinkle them with salt, and let them remain for a few minutes. When the bitter juice is drawn from them, fry them a nice colour on both sides in the remaining fat from the meat, then arrange them tastefully over the meat, or round the dish, sprinkle a little pepper over, and serve hot.

Kavurmalı Patlıcan

MUTTON FRICASSEED WITH EGGPLANTS II

Ingredients

3 lb mutton meat
3-4 eggplants
1/2 pint of broth

Cut in pieces the same quantity of mutton, and fry them in the same way as above; then bake in oven three or four medium sized eggplants. When soft, peel

Salt
Pepper
2 pinches cinnamon

them; then lay them in a pan, over which place the pieces of meat with the fat that is left from it in the stew pan; add half a pint of broth (No. 1); put the pan on a slow charcoal fire with the cover over, and let it simmer for twenty minutes; then dish up carefully, sprinkle a little cinnamon and pepper over, and serve while hot.

Paça

SHEEP'S TROTTERS WITH EGG-SAUCE

Ingredients

10 sheep's trotters
4 cloves of garlic
1/2 teacup of wine vinegar or juice of 4 lemons
2 eggs
2 lemons
Salt
Pepper
2 pinches cinnamon

Get already cleaned sheep's trotters; break the long bones and put them in a stew pan nearly full of water and place it on the fire or in a very hot oven, with the cover over it, until the meat comes off the bones. When done, take out the large bones, and cut the meat in small pieces. Then well pound garlic cloves in a mortar with a little salt; add wine vinegar, or the juice of lemons, and stir it well with a wooden spoon. Then pour it over the trotters, with a little salt. Stir it once, set it on the fire let it boil again for two or three minutes. Then lay on the bottom of a dish some thin slices of toast, over which place the pieces of trotters with some of the liquor, and put it on a very slow charcoal fire until the liquor is nearly absorbed. Then beat up the egg yolks with the lemon juice, and a little of the liquor in which the trotters are cooked. Place them on a moderate fire, and begin stirring with a wooden spoon (taking it from the fire now and then when getting too hot) until it thickens. Then pour it over the trotters, sprinkle a little pepper and cinnamon over, and serve very hot.

İmam bayıldı / Eggplant with Onions

İmam Bayıldı

EGGPLANT WİTH ONIONS

Ingredients

6 eggplants
5 onions
1/2 cup olive oil or 1/2 lb butter
6 cloves of garlic
1 pint of water
Salt

Cut the eggplants in four lengthways, without separating from the stalk; sprinkle them with salt, and let them remain for five or ten minutes. Peel and cut onions in rather thick slices, and fry them partly brown in olive oil or fresh butter. Then lay half of them on the bottom of a stew pan, over which place the eggplants, and lay the other half of the onions over them; add garlic, and a pint of water.

Put the pan on the fire, and let it simmer until the eggplants are soft. Then dish them up carefully, and serve hot or cold.

Vegetable marrow may be done in the same way.

Ekşili Patlıcan

SOUR EGGPLANTS

Ingredients

4 eggplants
1/2 cup olive oil
or 1/2 lb butter
4 onions (sliced)
1/2 teacup wine vinegar
1/2 tbls sugar
Salt

Cut eggplants in rather thin slices lengthwise; sprinkle them with some salt, and let them remain until the bitter juice is drawn from them. Then fry them a nice colour in olive oil, or in fresh butter, and lay them in a pan. Then fry nice brown sliced onions in fresh butter or olive oil, with a little salt, and lay them over the eggplants. Add wine vinegar, and sugar; set the pan on a moderate fire until the liquor is nearly absorbed, then dish them up carefully, and serve.Vegetable-marrow may be done in the same way.

Musakka

MINCED MUTTON DONE WITH EGGPLANT

Ingredients

2 lb mutton meat
4 eggplants
3 onions (chopped fine)
2 ounces butter
3 tbls parsley (chopped)
1 pint of broth no.1

Mince raw mutton or lamb; put it in a frying-pan with onions, butter, and a little salt. Set it on the fire and let the meat and the onions stew a nice brown, stirring it now and then. Two minutes before taking it off, add parsley, and stir it well. Then cut eggplants in slices lengthwise, and place them in salt water for ten or fifteen minutes. Place the minced meat and the eggplants in layers into a pan add a pint of broth (No. 1). Put the pan on a moderate charcoal fire with the cover over, and let it simmer until the liquor is nearly absorbed, and the eggplants are nicely cooked. When done, turn it on to a dish, without spoiling the shape, and serve. Artichokes and vegetable marrow may be cooked in the same way.

PART IX.

Dolmalar
Dishes Stuffed with Minced Meat, Rice

Dolmalar / Dishes Stuffed

Patlıcan Dolması

STUFFED EGGPLANTS

Ingredients

6 eggplants
1 lb mutton
1 lb mutton rib bones
2 onions (chopped fine)
5 eggs
1/2 cup rice
1/2 lbs butter
1 pint of broth
2 lemons
Salt
Pepper

Remove the stalks of the eggplants and cut off the tops as large as a two-shilling piece. Then take out the insides without making a hole at the other end, and throw them in salt water for ten or fifteen minutes. Then mince fine raw mutton, add well-washed rice, onions, sufficient salt and pepper, and mix them together with your hands. Stuff the eggplants with these ingredients, and cover them with the tops contrariwise. Then beat up the eggs in a basin, in which dip the eggplants, and fry them in hot fresh butter. Then prick them here and there with a fork, and place them in a stew pan, the bottom of which you have previously covered with rib-bones, so as to prevent them from burning while they are cooking. Cover them either with broth (No. 1.) or water, add the juice of lemons. Set it on a charcoal fire, and let it simmer till the liquor is nearly absorbed, or until it forms nice thick gravy at the bottom.

Then dish them up carefully, and serve hot. If you fancy, beat up two or three eggs with the gravy of the above, and the juice of half a lemon in a saucepan; place it on a very slow fire, and keep stirring. When it begins to thicken, pour over the eggplants, and then serve.

When you have stuffed the eggplants, you may first boil them until cooked, and then fry them. This is also a nice way, and will vary the flavour.

Vegetable-marrow and cucumbers may be cooked in the same way.

Yalancı Balık Dolması

CROOKED STUFFED FISH

Ingredients

6 eggplants
4 onions (chopped fine)
1/2 lbs rice
2 cup hot water
2 tbls pine nuts
1 tbls currants
Salt
Pepper
Mixed spice
1 lb mutton rib bone
1 cup olive oil
or 1/2 lb butter

Get rather thin and long eggplants, peel them very thin in spots here and there (imitating the fish scales) then cut off the tops, as large as a florin, and take out the whole of the inside, leaving only sufficient to bear stuffing. Throw them in salt water for ten or fifteen minutes. Then put nice olive oil or butter in a saucepan, and set it on the fire. When hot, add onions, and begin stirring it with a wooden spoon.

When on the point of browning, add good washed rice, and keep stirring. As soon as the rice begins to brown, pour in half a teacup of hot water, and continue stirring. When the water is absorbed, add another half a teacup of water, and keep stirring. When the rice is partly soft, add two ounces of pine nuts, currants, salt, pepper, and a little mixed spice. Stir well and then take it off.

When partly cold, stuff the eggplants with it, and cover them with the tops crosswise. Cover the bottom of a saucepan with some rib bones of mutton, and place the eggplants over.

Cover them with water, set the pan on the fire with the lid over, and let it simmer till the eggplants are partly soft. Then take them out and fry them a nice colour in hot olive oil or fresh butter; then dish them up tastefully, and serve.

Piyazlı Kabak

STUFFED VEGETABLE-MARROW

Ingredients

8 vegetable marrows
1 lb cheese (grated)
2 tbls parsley (chopped)
1/2 tbls mint (chopped)
3 eggs
1/2 lb butter
1/2 cup of broth

Peel very thin the vegetable-marrows and take out the insides, then stuff them with some nice cheese, grated and mixed with parsley, and mint. Then beat up eggs, in which dip the vegetable-marrow, and fry them a nice brown in hot fresh butter.

Then take them out and place them in a stew pan, cover them with broth (No. 1.), set the pan on a charcoal fire, and let it boil gently, until the liquor is nearly absorbed. Then dish up, and serve.

Halep Dolması

STUFFED EGGPLANTS SYRIAN STYLE

Ingredients

6 eggplants
1 lb mutton
2 onions
1/2 tbls mint
1 pinch saffron
4 tbls rice
1 lb mutton rib-bones
1/2 pint of broth
3 lemons

Cut off the tops and take out the insides eggplants, as Patlıcan Dolması, put them in salt water for ten minutes or so; then mince mutton, add onions, mint, saffron, two or three tablespoons of the inside of eggplants, all chopped fine, well washed rice, a little salt and pepper, mix them well all together with your hands. Then stuff the eggplants with it, and cover them with the tops. Then lay some rib-bones of mutton on the bottom of a stew pan, and place the eggplants over carefully. Cover them with broth (No. 1.), add the juice of the lemons, set the pan on a charcoal fire with the cover over, and let it simmer until the eggplants are soft, and a nice gravy is formed at the bottom.

Then dish them up carefully, and serve. When you take out the insides of the egg-plants, leave only sufficient to bear the stuffing. Instead of covering the stuffed egg-plants with broth and lemon juice, they cover them sometimes with juice.

Yalancı Dolma

STUFFED VINE-LEAVES

Ingredients

1/4 lb vine leaves
3/4 pint olive oil
1 lb mutton rib bones
2 1/2 lbs onions
(chopped fine)
21/2 lb rice
2 teacup water
2 ts mint (powdered)
Salt
Pepper
2 pinches cinnamon

Procure seven or eight dozens of young vine leaves, and seal them. Let them drain in a colander. Pour in a saucepan olive oil and place it on the fire. When hot, put in onions, and stir until they begin to brown. Then add two pounds and a half of the best rice, well cleaned, and keep stirring. When the rice is on the point of browning, add two teacups of water, and continue stirring gently until the water is absorbed; then take it off, add mint, a little salt, pepper, and cinnamon, and well stir it.

Then spread the vine leaves out, and put half a tablespoon of the prepared rice in each one, fold it about the length of your thumb, but a little thicker, and squeeze it gently in your hand, so that it may not open while cooking. When all ready, cover the bottom of a saucepan with rib bones of mutton, as Patlıcan Dolması (see p.97), and over which place the stuffed leaves one by one, arranging, at the same time, between them eight or ten sour plums. When the whole is laid, press them with a plate, then nearly cover them with water, and set the pan on the fire. When boiling, let it simmer until there is no liquid remaining; then take one out and try if the rice is soft; if not, add some more water. When soft, and each grain is separate, dish them up tastefully, and serve.

The object of placing unripe plums between the stuffed leaves is to give to them a slight acidity, which improves the flavour; and sometimes a small bunch of unripe grapes is placed over. They are preferred to lemon when they are in season. Only one half of this quantity need be made.

Kavun Dolması

STUFFED MUSK-MELON

Ingredients

1 musk-melon
2 onions (chopped fine)
1 lb mutton meat
1/2 lb butter
1/2 teacup rice
1 tbls currants
3 tbls almonds
3 tbls pine nuts

Procure a musk-melon, or any other one; cut out the part where the stalk is, twice the size of a crown piece, so as to form a lid; take out the seeds, and part of the inside; then fry a nice brown raw minced mutton in fresh butter, with onions and add well cleaned rice, sufficient salt and pepper, currants, skinned almonds, skinned, and pine nuts. Stir three or four minutes longer, and take it off; then stuff the melon with this mixture. Put the piece over that you have previously cut out for a lid, and pit it round with a few wooden pins; then put it in a baking-dish, and bake it nicely in the oven; then dish it up, and serve.

Sweet pumpkin may be done in the same way. If the pumpkin is not sweet, half a teacup of honey is added.

Yaprak Dolması / Ordinary Stuffed Vine-Leaves

Tavuk Dolması
STUFFED CHICKEN

Ingredients

1 chicken
1/2 lb butter
3/4 lb rice
3 tbls pine nuts
1 tbls currants
1 teacup hot water
1 pint of broth no.1 or no.2
Salt
Pepper
2 pinches cinnamon

Clean the chicken and sprinkle a little salt over, let it remain for ten minutes or so; then chop up the liver, heart, and the gizzards, very fine. Place them in a frying-pan with 2 table spoons of fresh butter and add well-washed rice, pine nuts, currants, sufficient salt and pepper, and a little cinnamon, stir round for a few minutes. Then add a small teacup of hot water, and keep stirring till the water is absorbed and the rice partly soft. Then stuff the chickens with it, sew them up, and fry them a nice brown in fresh butter;

then place them in a stew pan, nearly cover them with broth , put the pan on a charcoal fire with the cover over, and let it simmer till the chicken is quite tender. Dish up, and serve.

This receipt is applicable to all kinds of birds, game, or poultry, only turkey and goose are first scalded for a few minutes, and when placed in a stew pan to simmer, they are covered with the liquor in which they are scalded.

Yaprak Dolması

ORDINARY STUFFED VINE-LEAVES

Ingredients

1/4 lb vine leaves
1 lb mutton
2 onions (peeled)
4 tbls rice
1 pint of broth no.1
Salt
Pepper

Prepare some vine leaves as Yalancı Dolma (see p.100); then chop up fine raw mutton with one or two onions, add well washed rice, a little salt and pepper, and mix them well together with a little water, to make it like a paste. Then lay the vine leaves open, put in each one a teaspoonful of this stuffing, and wrap them up about the length and the thickness of your thumb; squeeze them gently with your hand one by one, that they may retain the stuffing while cooking. Then place them in a saucepan without any water, and set it on the fire with the cover over. When their own moisture is exhausted, add broth (No. 1), and let it simmer until it forms a nice gravy at the bottom. Then take one out and try if the meat and the rice are done; if not, add some more broth. When the rice and the meat are quite tender, dish up, and serve.

Şalgam Dolması
STUFFED TURNIPS

Ingredients

6 turnips
1 lb mutton
2 onions (chopped fine)
2 tbls rice
1 pint of broth
2 tbls wine vinegar
1 tbls sugar
Salt
Pepper

Peel middle-sized turnips, and hollow them out exactly as Kavun Dolması; then mince raw mutton, add onions, parsley, and a handful of well-cleaned rice, and a little salt and pepper, mix well all together with the hands. Then stuff the turnips with it, and place the lids over as above.

Place them in a stew pan, and nearly cover them with broth (No. 1); add a little salt; put the pan on the fire with the cover over, and let it simmer until the turnips are nearly soft, then add wine vinegar, and sugar. When sufficient gravy is left, and the turnips are quite done, dish up tastefully, and serve.

Domates Dolması
STUFFED TOMATOES

Ingredients

24 tomatoes
1 lb mutton
2 onions (peeled)
4 tbls rice
Salt
Pepper
1 pint of broth no.1

Procure either ripe on unripe tomatoes, cut off the tops about the size of a shilling, but without separating them, so as to form lids, take out the seeds and part of the inside; then prepare some stuffing as above, stuff them, and close the lids.

Place them carefully in a stew pan, and nearly cover them with broth (No. 1), put the pan on the fire, and let it simmer till sufficient gravy is left; then dish up tastefully, and serve.

Yalancı Patlıcan Dolması
STUFFED EGGPLANTS CROOKED

Ingredients

6 eggplants
1 teacup olive oil
1/2 lbs onions (chopped fine)
1 lbs rice
1 tbls mint (chopped fine)
1 pint+1teacup of water
Salt
Pepper

Prepare the eggplants as Patlıcan Dolması (see p.97). Then sprinkle some salt over the insides of the eggplants. After a few minutes squeeze them well with your hands, to be free from bitter water, and chop them up. Then put a teacup of olive oil in a saucepan, place it on the fire. When hot, put in onions, and stir until they begin to brown. Then add the insides of the eggplants, and stir for three minutes or so. Add well-washed rice, sufficient salt and pepper, mint, and water. Keep stirring until the moisture is absorbed, then stuff the eggplants moderately with it, put the lids over. Then prick them here and there with a fork, place them in a saucepan, and nearly cover them with water, set it on the fire with the cover over, and let it boil gently until the liquor is absorbed; then dish up, and serve hot or cold.

Mumbar ve Şirdan
FRESH SAUSAGE

Ingredients

1 ventricle or intestine of sheep
1 lb mutton
2 teacups rice
1/2 lbs butter

Get some ventricle or intestine of sheep well cleaned and ready for use. Then mince mutton, add well washed rice, sufficient salt and pepper, a little cinnamon, and mix them well together with a little water, to form it like a paste. Then tie one end of the ventricle and stuff it with the

Salt
Pepper
2 pinches cinnamon

minced meat through a funel;then tie the other end and prick it all over with a needle. When ready, nearly fill a saucepan with water and sufficient salt, and place it on the fire.

When boiled, throw in the stuffed ventricle; and when partly cooked, take it out and place it on a trencher; then twist it round and round to form it like a twisted bun. When cold, fry it a nice colour in hot fresh butter, and serve. If approved of, cut it in thin slices, dip them in egg, and then fry them in butter, and serve.

The stuffing can also be made from the lamb's or sheep's heart and lights, chopped up fine with one or two onions, and prepared as above.

Midye Dolması
STUFFED MUSSELS

Ingredients

48 mussels
1/2 pint olive oil
3 onions (chopped fine)
1 lb rice
2 tbls pine nuts
1 tbls currants
Salt
Pepper
Mixed spice
Water

Scrape the mussels' shells in water, wash them several times, and open them with a knife without separating one form the other. Then put half a pint of olive oil in a saucepan, with onions, and set it on the fire. When hot, begin to stir with a wooden spoon until the onions are nicely browned; then add well washed rice, pine nuts, and currants, a little salt and pepper, and mixed spice. Stir till the rice begins to brown, then add a teacup of water, and keep stirring until the moisture is dispersed; then take it off. When nearly cold, stuff the mussels, and close the shells.

Then arrange them in a stew pan, nearly cover them with water, place a plate over, inside downwards, set the pan on the fire with the cover over, and let it boil until the whole of the liquid is absorbed. Then dish up carefully, and serve hot or cold.

Balık Dolması

STUFFED FISH

Ingredients

4 mackerel
1 cup olive oil
3 onions (chopped fine)
2 tbls pine nuts
1 tbls currants
3 tbl flour
1 egg (beaten)
Salt
Pepper
Mixed spice

Get medium sized Mackerel, or whiting, or any other fish you may fancy, well clean them, and take out the gills, break the bones of the tails, and skin them, without tearing the skin, in one piece, and the head must be attached to the skin.

Then remove the flesh from the bones, and chop it up. Put half a teacup of olive oil in a frying pan, place it on the fire. When hot, put in onions, and stir them with a wooden spoon until nicely browned. Then add the fish, pine nuts, currants, a little pepper and salt, and a little mixed spice, and keep stirring until the fish is nearly done.

Then stuff the fish skins with it, dip them in flour, and then in egg, and fry them in hot olive oil till a nice colour, turning them over. When done, take them out with a slice carefully, let them drain.

Dish up on a white napkin, and serve.

PART X.

PİLAVLAR
PILAFF, OR RICE, COOKED WITH MEAT, &C., IN VARIOUS WAYS

Erişteli Pilav / Pilaff

Pirinç Pilavı

ORDINARY PILAFF

Ingredients

2 pints water
1 lb rice
2 ts salt
1/2 lb butter

Pour water in a saucepan, and put it on the fire. When boiling, throw in the best rice well washed, and salt, and boil it until the whole of the liquid is absorbed.

Then put in saucepan butter, and set it on the fire until it boils, then pour it all at once over the rice. Put the cover over the pan, wrap a wet cloth round it, to prevent the steam from escaping, and keep it on the hob for half an hour. Then take the lid off and stir it once round with a fork. You will find that each grain is swollen and is well separated. Then dish up in the shape of a dome, and serve hot.

Acem Pilavı

PILAFF PERSIAN FASHION

Ingredients

3 lb mutton
4 onions (chopped fine)
3 tbls pine nuts
3 tbls currants
2 lb rice
2 quarts of water
Salt
Mixed spice

Cut mutton in pieces about the size of walnuts, place them in a stew pan: if the meat is not fat, add three or four ounces of fresh butter; put the pan on a charcoal fire, and let the meat stew till quite brown, but not burnt, and the fat is as clear as oil, which you will easily see by holding the pan on one side.

Then take out the pieces of meat with a hand strainer, and put them in a basin. Then place onions in the remaining fat, and fry them a nice brown. Then lay the pieces of meat over, add pine nuts, currants, mixed spice, well washed rice, pour gently two quarts of cold water over, add sufficient salt, put the cover over the pan, and cement round it with flour paste, so as to keep the steam in. Put the pan on the fire, and let it boil gently until the whole of the liquid is absorbed.

Then take off the cover, and turn the contents of the pan carefully on to a hot dish, and serve.

This Pilaff is very pleasing to the sight, and exceedingly pleasant to the plate.

Kıymalı Pilav

PILAFF WITH MINCED MEAT

Ingredients

1 lb mutton
1/4 lb butter
1 lb rice
2 pints hot water
Salt
2 pinches cinnamon

Chop up the mutton meat and put it in a saucepan with butter, set it on the fire, and let the meat stew a nice brown.

Then add a pound of the best rice, well washed, two pints of hot water, sufficient salt, and a pinch or two of cinnamon, and let it boil slowly until there is no liquid remaining.

Then take it off and place it on the hob with the cover over for twenty or thirty minutes. Dish it up in a dome shape, and serve hot.

Mevlevi Pilavı

THE PILAFF OF DANCING DERVISH

Ingredients

1 lb rice
2 quarts water
1/2 lb butter
Salt

Put water in a saucepan with salt and put it on the fire. When boiling, throw into it well washed rice, and boil until each grain is soft and separate.

Then drain it through a clean cloth or in a colander, put it back in the pan, and set it on a slow fire without the cover until the moisture is dispersed. Then put a saucepan on the fire with half a pound of fresh butter.

When it boils, pour it over the rice and stir it once round with o fork, put the pan on the hob with the cover over, and let it remain for five or ten minutes. Dish up, and serve hot.

Susuz Pilav

PILAFF DONE WITHOUT WATER

Ingredients

2 lb mutton or lamb
2 1/2 lb rice
1/2 lb butter (melted)
6 pieces of gum mastic
1 ts salt
1 ts pepper
2 pinches cinnamon

Cut mutton or lamb meat into pieces the size of walnuts, wash them, sprinkle them with sufficient salt and pepper, and lay them on the bottom of a stew pan (the cover of which must fit tight). Then well wash rice, and place it over the meat; then pour hot fresh butter over, add gum-mastic, cinnamon, put the cover over the pan contrariwise, wrap a wet cloth round it, and fill the cover with water. Set the pan on a slow charcoal fire, and let it simmer for about four hours. When done take off the cover, turn the contents carefully on to a hot dish, and serve.

Altın Nohutlu Pilav / Pilaff

Domates Pilavı

PILAFF DONE WITH TOMATO

Ingredients

1 lb rice
2 onions (chopped fine)
1/2 lb butter
1 pint tomato juice
1 pint of broth
Salt
Pepper

Fry a nice brown onions in 2 table spoons fresh butter. Then put them in a saucepan with tomato juice, which you have previously passed through a cloth or a sieve, broth (No. 1), and sufficient salt, and put the pan on the fire. When boiling, add well washed rice, and let it boil gently till the liquor is absorbed; then put on the fire a saucepan with a quarter of a pound of fresh butter. When very hot, pour it over the rice, stir it once round with a fork, put the cover over the pan, and let it remain on the hob for fifteen or twenty minutes. Dish it up, sprinkle a pinch of pepper over, and serve.

Tavuk Pilavı
PILAFF WITH CHICKEN

Ingredients

1 chicken
11/2 lb rice
3/4 lb butter
6 pieces of gum mastic
3 pinches of cinnamon
Salt

Place the chicken in a saucepan, and nearly fill it with water, add a little salt, and set it on the fire. When boiling, skim and simmer until the chicken is tender; then take it out, place it in a dish, and keep it hot.

Then measure three pints of the broth of the chicken, and pour it in a pan, to which add well washed rice, butter, gum mastic, cinnamon, and half a teaspoonful of salt.

Put the pan on the fire with the cover over, and let it boil gently until the liquor is absorbed. Then take it off, stir it once round with a fork, and keep it on the hob with the cover over for fifteen or twenty minutes. Each grain will then swell up and be well separated. Dish up the rice, in the centre of which place the chicken, cut in pieces, and serve very hot.Quails are very nice done in the same way.

Baş Pilavı
PILAFF DRESSED WITH LAMB'S BRAINS

Ingredients

2 lambs head
1 1/2 lb rice
1/4 lb butter
6 pieces gum mastic
Pepper
2 pinches cinnamon

Wash lambs' heads well, and place them in a stew pan nearly full of water, add sufficient salt, and put the pan on the fire. When boiling, skim and simmer until the meat comes off the heads; then cut them open, take out the brains, put them in a basin, and beat them up with a little broth of the heads to the thickness of a thick cream.

Then pass the broth through a sieve, measure three pints of it into a saucepan, add a quarter of a pound of fresh butter (if it is not rich), a little pepper, ground cinnamon, and gum mastic, and set the pan on the fire. As soon as boiling commences, add well washed rice, and let it simmer until the liquor is absorbed. Then take it off, and place it on the hob for ten minutes or so, then dish it up in the shape of a dome, spread the brain all over, then brown it nicely in the oven, and serve.

This Pilaff is considered very pleasant and most nutritious.

Yağsız Pilav
PILAFF WITHOUT BUTTER

Ingredients

1 chicken
1 lb rice
2 pieces of cinnamon stick (ca. 3 cm)
3 pieces of gum mastic

Put the chicken in a saucepan nearly full of water, and sufficient salt, and set it on the fire. When boiling, skim and simmer until the meat separates from the bones; then take it off, and pass the whole through a clean cloth or sieve by pressing and squeezing it with your hand, and cast the residue away. Then put in the saucepan two measures of the liquor to one of well-washed rice, add cinnamon, and gum mastic; set it on a charcoal fire till the liquor is absorbed. Then take it off, and place it on the hob, stir it once round with a fork, and let it remain covered for fifteen minutes or so. Then take out the pieces of cinnamon, dish up, and serve hot. This is the most delicious pilaf, and it is light.

Patlıcan Pilavı

PILAFF MADE WITH EGGPLANT

Ingredients

4 eggplants
3/4 lb butter
2 onions (chopped)
2 pint hot water
1 pint of broth
3 pieces gum mastic
1 pinch saffron
11/2 lb rice
Salt
Pepper

Cut the eggplants in four crosswise, take out the insides, if seeded, and cut them in slices about an inch thick. Then scald them in salt water, and drain them. Put butter in a saucepan with onions; put it on the fire, and let the onions stew. When nearly brown, add the pieces of eggplants, and fry them partly together with the onions. Then add hot water, and broth (No. 1), a little salt and pepper, gum mastic, and saffron. As soon as it boils, add rice, and let it boil slowly until the liquor is absorbed; then take it off, and place it on the hob for ten minutes or so. Dish it up, and serve.

Hünkâr Pilavı

IMPERIAL PILAFF

Ingredients

2 lb rice
2 1/2 lb mutton meat
4 pints water
1/2 lb butter
3 tbls pine nuts
3 tbls minced meat
3 tbls currants
1/2 ts mixed spice
Salt

Wash the rice, put it in a clean cloth, tie it, and hang it up; then cut mutton in pieces about the size of walnuts, wash and place them in a stew pan with water, and put it on a charcoal fire. When boiling, skim it well, add sufficient salt, and let it simmer for twenty or thirty minutes; then drain the liquor into o basin, put butter over the pieces of meat, and fry them a nice brown. Then add three pints of the liquor, with a little salt, pine nuts stanchions, minced raw mutton, previously fried a nice colour in fresh butter, currants, and half a teaspoon of mixed spice. As soon as it boils boil it for two or three minutes longer; then reduce the heat of the fire by removing the burning coals, and leaving only the ashes and the sparks. Put on the pan with the cover over about an hour; then dish up tastefully, and serve.

Domatesli Bulgur Pilavı / Pilaff with Tomato

Balık Pilavı

PILAF DONE WITH FISH

Ingredients

1 lb rice
1 lb fish
1 1/2 teacup olive oil
2 pints water
Salt
2 pinches cinnamon

Put olive oil in a stew pan, and set it on the fire. As soon as it begins to bubble, pour into it carefully two pints of water, with a little salt. When boiling, add well-washed rice; then lay over any fish you choose, previously well cleaned and seasoned with salt; put the cover over the pan, and let it simmer until the liquor is absorbed. Then take it off, and place it on the hob for fifteen minutes or so.

Then dish up the rice, and place fish over tastefully, sprinkle a little cinnamon over, and serve hot.

Midye Pilavı

PILAF MADE WITH MUSSELS

Ingredients

1 lb rice
48 mussels
3 onions (chopped)
3 tomatoes or 2 tbls tomato paste
1/2 pint olive oil
2 1/2 pints water
Salt

Put olive oil in a saucepan with onions and set it on the fire until the onions are nicely browned, stirring them now and then. Then add the tomatoes, cut in four crossways: if not in season, two tablespoons of tomato sauce will answer. Place the mussels with their shells open, but not separated one from another, and well scraped and washed, water, and sufficient salt. When boiling, add well washed rice, put the cover over the pan, and let it simmer until the liquor is absorbed. Then take it off, and place it on the hob for twenty minutes or so. Dish up, and serve hot or cold.

Tarak Pilavı

PILAFF COOKED WITH SCALLOPS

Ingredients

1 lb rice
36 scallops
6 ounces butter
3 onions (chopped fine)
1/2 teacup olive oil
Salt
Pepper

Wash the scallops well and scrape the shells and open them without separating one from the other; then put butter in a pan, with onions; set it on the fire, and fry them partly brown.

Then add well washed rice, a little salt and pepper, and stir it with a wooden spoon for ten minutes or so. Then stuff the scallops with the rice, and place them carefully in a convenient saucepan, with olive oil, cover them with water, put a plate over upside downwards, put the lid on, and let it simmer on a moderate fire until there is no liquid remaining; then arrange them in a dish, and serve, hot or cold.

This may also be cooked in the same way as Pilaff made with mussels.

PART XI.

SICAK HAMUR TATLILARI
HOT SWEET PASTRY

Baklava ve Tatlılar / Sweet Pastry

Baklava

A DISH OF FLAKY PASTRY "BAKLAVA"

Ingredients

Thin pie pastry (p.79)
1 cup wheat starch
1 lb butter
1 lb almonds or pistachios or hazelnuts
1 lb honey or sugar
2 pints water
1 lb sugar

Divide the pastry into fifty pieces the size of walnuts, sprinkle a little wheat starch under and over, and roll them out with a rolling-pin as thin as tissue paper, quite round, and the size of the baking-tin you intend to lay them in. Then butter the tin(1), in which lay five of the pieces of paste one over the other, sprinkle a little fresh butter over the top one, and lay five more pieces over; then sprinkle either pounded almonds, pistachios, or hazelnuts, all over, and lay five more pieces of paste over, butter again, and five more pieces of paste; then either of the above ingredients, and five more pieces of paste over, butter again, and so forth, until you have laid all the pieces of paste.

Then cut it up in diamonds, pour about half a pound or a little more of scalded fresh butter all over, and bake it a nice colour in a hot oven.

Syrup: While it is baking, put honey or sugar into a saucepan, with water, and set it to boil until it becomes syrup.

When the paste is nicely browned, pour it gently all over, and let it remain for five minutes or so. Then dish up in pyramid, sprinkle some powdered sugar over, and serve hot or cold.

1) In Turkey the baking-tins are made of copper from two to three inches deep. They are circular, and from one to two feet in diameter.

Kaymaklı Baklava
BAKLAVA WITH CLOTTED CREAM

Ingredients

50 sheet of Baklava pastry (p. 123)
2 lb clotted cream
1/3 lb butter
4 eggs
1 lb honey or sugar
2 pints water

Prepare Baklava pastry, and lay half of them in a baking-tin, sprinkling a little scalded fresh butter between each piece. Put in a basin the egg whites, divide the cream in pieces, rub them with the white of eggs both under and over with a quill or a paste-brush, and lay them all over the pastry. Then cover them with the remaining pieces of pastry, sprinkling butter between each as before. Then cut it in diamonds or any other shape you fancy; and bake it a delicate colour. Pour some syrup over as above, and serve.

The object of rubbing the cream with the white of egg is to prevent it from melting while the paste is baking. Or you may bake one half of the pieces of paste in one tin, and the other half in another tin.

When done, pour the syrup over both, then laid the cream over one, and cover it with the other, cut it up as above, and serve. Alternatively, beat up the cream with a little milk and the white of two or three eggs, lay it between the pieces of pastry, and then bake it.

Süslü Kaymak Baklavası

"BAKLAVA" CROOKED CREAM PASTRY

Ingredients

50 sheet of Baklava pastry (p. 123)
1 1/2 cups ground rice
3 cups milk
1/3 lb butter
2 eggs
1 lb honey or sugar
2 pints water

Lay half of the pastry in baking-tin as above; then boil ground rice with milk until reduced to a thick pulp. When cold, put it in a basin with the egg whites, and work it with your hands for five or ten minutes, or until you bring it to the thickness of clotted cream. Then lay it all over the pastry, and cover it with the remaining pieces of it. Cut it up in diamonds, and bake it and pour the syrup over as above. Dish up tastefully, sprinkle sugar over, and serve.

Cream cheese worked with a little powdered sugar may be used instead of rice.

Kavun Baklavası

BAKLAVA WITH MELON

Ingredients

40 sheets of Baklava pastry
1/3 lb butter
1 musk melon
Syrup (p. 123)

Butter a baking-tin, in which lay 20 sheets of pastry, sprinkling scalded fresh butter between each one.

Then peel a small musk-melon, or any other sweet melon, cut it in two, take out the seeds, mash one half or the whole of the melon with a wooden spoon, then lay it all over the paste half an inch thick, cover it twenty sheets of paste as before; and bake it a nice colour. When done, and while hot, shake some powdered sugar over, and serve.

Pirinç Baklavası

A KIND OF GROUND RICE PUDDING

Ingredients

1 lb ground rice
1 pint honey
1 lb butter
1 pint hot water
1 ts carbonate of soda
Syrup (see p. 123)

Put in a clean stew pan the honey, which you have previously boiled and skimmed, the butter, previously melted, hot water, ground rice, and a carbonate of soda dissolved in three tablespoons of water; put the pan on a charcoal fire, and stir it until reduced to a thick pulp.

Then pour it in a lightly-buttered baking-tin, spread it all over with a spoon, and bake it a nice brown in a hot oven. When done, cut it up in diamonds, sprinkle powdered sugar over, dish up in pyramid, and serve. If honey is not fancied, use a pound of sugar previously dissolved in water, and boiled to the consistency of syrup.

Revani

SAGO PUDDING OR CAKE

Ingredients

2 1/8 lb sago
1 1/4 butter
12 eggs
1 1/4 cup sugar
3/4 lb sugar
7 pints water
4 tbls powdered sugar

Put in a basin fresh butter, and work it well with clean hands until it is like a cream; then break in the eggs, and beat up well together; then mix sugar, and while beating up, add gradually sago [1] and keep beating it up for a few minutes longer. Then butter a rather deep baking-tin, in which pour the preparation, and bake it a nice colour in a hot oven. Then dissolve sugar in water, and keep it lukewarm. When the pudding is nicely browned, pour gradually some of the sherbet or sugar and water all over with a ladle, put itagain in the oven until the sherbet is absorbed, and continue in this manner until you have used the whole of the sherbet; then cut it up in diamonds, dish up tastefully, shake some powdered sugar over, and serve.

1) In Turkey the sago is made of plain paste in grains as small as gun powder.

Revani II

SAGO PUDDING OR CAKE

Ingredients

2 1/2 lb sago
1 1/4 lb butter
6 eggs
2 1/2 lb honey
2 pint of water
6 ounces of sugar
3 pints of water
1/2 teacup rosewater
4 tbls powdered sugar

Prepare butter as above, break eggs over, and beat up well together, to which add honey and beat them up well; then add by degrees the sago (see Revani) bringing it to the consistency of a thick batter.

Then pour it in a rather deep baking-tin, previously buttered, and bake it a nice brown in a hot oven; then dissolve sugar in water, with rosewater, and keep it lukewarm.

When the pudding is nicely done, pour it all over, and put it again in the oven.

When the whole of the liquid is absorbed, take it out, cut it up in any shape you fancy, dish up, and serve with powdered sugar over.

Kadın Göbeği

LADY'S NAVEL

Ingredients

2 3/4 lb flour
3/4 lb butter
Syrup (see p. 123)
1 ts carbonate of soda
Salt

Put in a stew pan fresh butter, and set it on the fire. When melted, mix in by degrees the flour, and keep stirring until the flour is partly browned. It should be a nice gold colour. Then take it out, and place it on a pastry slab, make a hole in the centre, in which put a teaspoon of salt, mix it with water (in which a teaspoon of carbonate of soda is dissolved previously) into a softly paste with your hands, then form it into small cakes, and make a dent in the centre of each one with the point of your finger.

Place them in a buttered tin, and bake them a nice colour; then have ready some syrup as in "Baklava". When the cakes are nicely done, pour it over; put it again in the oven, or on a slow charcoal fire until the syrup is absorbed.

Dish up tastefully, and serve.

Süngeriye

SPONGE PUDDING

Ingredients

40 eggs
3/4 lb ground rice
2 drops rose essence
5 pints of milk
Syrup (see p. 123)

Put in a basin the white of forty eggs, and beat them up until they are formed into a firm froth; then add by degrees ground rice, with a few drops of the essence of rose, or any other essence you fancy, and heat it up again for some time. Then put into a saucepan the milk, and set it on a charcoal fire. When boiling, throw in a tablespoon of the mixture at a time, which will be done in a few minutes;take it out with a hand-strainer, and throw it into boiling syrup, which you have previously prepared, of sugar and water as above, take it out again with the hand-strainer after a few seconds, and place it in a dish.

Continue in this manner until the whole is done, and serve.

Kurabiye
SMALL CAKES

Ingredients

4 lb flour
2 1/2 lb butter
2 1/2 lb sugar

Put in a basin or pan melted fresh butter, with sugar, and stir it well; then add the flour. Knead it well, and make it into small cakes; place them in a buttered tin, and bake a nice colour in the oven. Half, or even a quarter of this quantity may be made.

Kurabiye II
SMALL CAKES II

Ingredients

2 lb flour
1 3/8 lb butter
1 lb sugar
1 nutmeg (grated)

Put in a saucepan fresh butter, and set it on the fire. When melted, mix in gradually flour, and stir until the flour is done; then take it off, and while it is getting cold, beat it up till it becomes a smooth substance; then add by degrees sugar, and a finely-grated nutmeg. Then work it well with your hands, and make it into small cakes, any fanciful shape you please, place them in a buttered tin, and bake a delicate colour in the oven.

These can be kept for a year without fear of their being spoiled.

Lokum

A KIND OF CAKES

Ingredients

1 3/8 ounces flour
3/4 lb butter
3/4 pint of water
10 eggs

Put fresh butter in a saucepan, and set it on the fire. When hot, add flour, and keep stirring till it becomes a light brown. Then pour water over, and continue stirring until it becomes like a paste; then take it off and let it remain till cold. Then add about the eggs, and work it with your hands to form a softly paste; then divide it in round pieces the size of small peaches, hollow the centre of each with the point of your finger, lay them in a buttered baking-tin, and bake them a nice delicate colour.

When done, fill them with the jam (see Vişne Reçeli p.205), or any other jam, clotted cream, or minced meat, previously stewed brown in fresh butter. Dish them up tastefully on a white napkin, and serve.

Lokum II

A KIND OF CAKES II

Malzeme

2 cups flour
1/2 lb butter
2 eggs
1/2 cup milk
2 pinches salt
4 tbls powdered sugar

Work lightly in a basin flour with 4 ounces fresh butter, add eggs, milk, and salt; work all well to form a nice paste. Then make it into small diamond-shaped cakes, and fry them a delicate colour in hot fresh butter; take them out and place them in a strainer. When free from grease, dish them up in crown or pyramid, shake some powdered sugar over, and serve.

Lokum III

A KIND OF CAKES III

Ingredients

1 lb flour
3/4 lb butter
3+1 eggs
4 tbls cream
3 tbls sugar
4 tbls powdered sugar
Salt

Work lightly in a basin flour, with scalded fresh butter, add eggs, cream, a little salt, sugar. Work all together well to form a nice stiff paste. Then make it into cakes, as above, or in any shape you please, arrange them in a buttered baking-tin, egg over, and bake a nice brown in the oven; sprinkle some powdered sugar over, and serve.

Sütlü Tel Kadayıf / A kind Fresh Vermicelli with milk

Tel Kadayıf

A SWEET DISH, PREPARED OF A KIND FRESH VERMICELLI

Ingredients

2 lb flour
3/4 lbs butter
1 lb sugar
4 pints of water

Procure a tin pint pot, the shape of a tumbler, insert in the bottom eight or ten fine tubes. Then put flour in a basin, mix it with water to form a smooth batter; put a portion of the batter in the pot, let it run through the tubes, by passing the pot up and down on a very hot crumpet-stove, which is done in a few minutes in long threads like vermicelli. Take them up, and spread them on a tray, and continue in this way till you have made about three pounds; then lay the vermicelli even in a buttered baking-tin, pour scalded fresh butter over, and bake it a nice brown on both sides in the oven, or on a charcoal fire.

Then put sugar in a stew pan, with two pints of water, and set it to boil until it becomes syrup; skim, and keep it hot.When the vermicelli is done, pour the syrup all over. If you wish it to be crisp, leave it uncovered; if soft, cover it the moment you have poured the syrup over, and let it remain for fifteen minutes or so; then cut it in four crossways, or any other shape you fancy, dish up. If any syrup is left in the baking tin, pour it over, and serve hot or cold.

Instead of making the vermicelli like strings, you can buy it from the shops. any other shape you fancy, dish up. If any syrup is left in the baking tin, pour it over, and serve hot or cold.

Çörek Kadayıf

THE SAME, PREPARED IN THE SHAPE OF TWISTED BUNS

Ingredients

3 lb vermicelli (see p.131)
1/2 lb butter
Syrup (see p.123)

Twist vermicelli like a rope, twice the thickness of your thumb, and make it into cakes the size of a Bath bun. Lay them in a buttered baking-tin, pour in scalded fresh butter, and bake it on both sides a nice brown. When done, pour some hot syrup all over, as above, and let it remain for ten minutes or so, dish up, and serve hot or cold.

Saray Tel Kadayıf

THE SAME, PALACE FASHION

Ingredients

3 lb vermicelli (see p.131)
1 lb butter
2 pint hot water
Syrup (see p.123)

Lay tel kadayıf in a rather deep baking-tin, about two inches thick, nearly cover it with scalded fresh butter, and bake it a nice colour on both sides in the oven. When done, strain the butter, and then pour hot water over to wash out all the fat; then pour hot syrup over. Put it again in the oven for five minutes or so; then cut it in four crossways, or in any fanciful shape you please, dish up, and serve hot or cold.

Kaymaklı Kadayıf

THE SAME, WITH CLOTTED CREAM

Ingredients

4 lb vermicelli (see p. 131)
1 lb butter

Prepare vermicelli, as Tel Kadayıf; lay half of it in a buttered baking-tin, and the other half in another buttered tin, pour in each about half a pound of scalded fresh

2 pint hot water
Clotted cream
Syrup (see p.123)

butter, and bake them a delicate colour on both sides. When cooked, strain and wash out all the butter from both, as above; then lay some clotted cream over one, half an inch thick, and cover it with the other one; then pour hot syrup all over, as Tel Kadayıf, and put it again in the oven until the syrup is nearly absorbed. Then cut it in any shape you fancy, or turn it on to a dish as it is, and serve.

Kaymaklı Kadayıf II
ANOTHER SORT

Ingredients

4 lb vermicelli (see p.131)
1/2 lb butter
2 pint hot water
3/4 lb clotted cream
7 ounces ground rice
Syrup (see p..123)

Make vermicelli, as Tel Kadayıf, lay half of it in a buttered baking-tin; then put in a basin clotted cream, and work it with six or seven ounces of ground rice. Then lay it all over the vermicelli, and cover it with the other half of vermicelli.

Pour in a little scalded butter, and bake it a nice brown on both sides; pour some syrup over, as above, and serve.

Yassı Kadayıf
A SWEET DISH MADE CRUMPETS

Ingredients

6 crumpets
1 lb sugar
2 pint of water
6 eggs
1/2 lb butter
3 tbls pistachios or almonds

Put sugar into a saucepan, with water, set it to boil until it becomes a syrupy, and keep it boiling gently by the side of the fire. Then beat up the eggs in a basin, in which dip the crumpets one after the other, and fry them a nice brown on both sides in scalded fresh butter. Then throw them in the syrup, take them out instantly and dish them up,

2 drops essence of rose or orange

sprinkling between each one some pounded pistachios or almonds; then put essence of rose or orange-flower in a teacup of water, and pour it over the crumpets, put it in the oven or on a slow charcoal fire for five minutes or so, and then serve.

Yassı Kadayıf II
ANOTHER KIND

Ingredients

6 crumpets
1/2 lb butter
1 cup powdered sugar
3 tbls pistachios or almonds
Rosewater

Fry the crumpets a nice colour in scalded fresh butter; whilst hot, arrange them in a dish, sprinkling between them powdered sugar, with pounded pistachios or almonds, and rosewater; let them remain covered for a few minutes, and serve.

Yağsız Kadayıf
THE SAME, WITHOUT BUTTER

Ingredients

8 crumpets
1 pint milk
1/2 cups powdered sugar
1/3 lb clotted cream

Lay half of the crumpets in a rather deep baking-tin, pour over them half of the milk, then sprinkle powdered sugar over, then a layer of clotted cream, and then an equal number of crumpets over.

Pour the rest of the milk, then sugar; put it on a charcoal fire, and let it boil for a little while, but take it off just before the cream is melted. When rather cold, dish them up carefully, shake some powdered sugar over, and serve.

Yufkalı Kadayıf

VERMICELLI WITH FLAKY PASTRY

Ingredients

6 sheets of puffy pastry
3 lb vermicelli (see p.131)
1/4 lb butter
Syrup (see p. 123)

Lay three of the pastry on the bottom of a well-buttered baking-tin, one over the other; then lay vermicelli (see Tel Kadayıf) over, about half or three-quarters of an inch thick; pour five or six tablespoons of scalded fresh butter all over, then cover it with a carving-fork, and bake it a nice brown on both sides. When done pour some syrup over, as Tel Kadayıf, and let it remain covered for ten minutes or so; cut it in diamonds, or any other fanciful shape you please; dish up tastefully, and serve.

Ekmek Kadayıfı

A SWEET DISH MADE OF MUFFINS

Ingredients

4 muffins
1 lb sugar
2 pint of water
6 tbls pistachios or almonds
1/3 lb clotted cream

Put sugar in a saucepan, with water, set it to boil until it becomes syrup. Then cut open the muffins, and put them in the syrup for two or three minutes, take them out carefully with a slice, lay half of them in a baking-tin, sprinkle some pounded pistachios or almonds over, then a layer of clotted cream over, a quarter of an inch thick, again pistachios or almonds, and cover them with the other half of the muffins. Then pour three-quarters of a pint of the syrup over, and put it in the oven, or on a moderate charcoal fire, until the syrup is nearly absorbed; dish up, and serve hot or cold.

Nuriye

A SWEET DISH, CALLED "SPLENDID"

Ingredients

1 lb flour
1 ts salt
5 eggs
3 lemons
1 lb butter (melted)
1/3 lb clotted cream
1/2 pint milk
1 teacup rose water
2 pinches cinnamon
Syrup *(See p..123)*

Put in a basin or on a slab the flour, make a hole in the center, and put a teaspoon of salt, egg whites, and the juice of the lemons strained, mix all together, then dip your hands in butter, and work it until it forms a softly flexible paste.

Then divide it in pieces the size of walnuts, roll them out to the thickness of a sixpence with a rolling-pin, fold each piece even. Then fry them a nice brown in scalded fresh butter and put them in a colander. When free from fat, throw them in boiling syrup, as in Tel Kadayıf; take them out, and lay half of them in a baking-tin, one over the other, then lay all over some clotted cream, about a quarter of an inch thick, and cover it with the other half of the paste.

Then add the milk, put it on a charcoal fire, and let it boil until quite soft. Then sprinkle some rosewater over, with a little powdered cinnamon, and serve.

Fodla Kadayıfı

ANOTHER SORT, MADE OF FRENCH ROLL

Ingredients

4 French rolls
3 eggs
1/2 lb butter
1 teacup rose water
Syrup *(See p.123)*

Cut the French rolls in slices lengthwise, about a quarter of an inch thick. Then beat up the eggs in a basin, in which dip the slices of bread, and fry them a nice delicate colour in scaled fresh butter, on both sides. When done, take them out with a slice, let them drain, and put them in hot syrup, which youhave previously made of sugar and water, as in Ekmek Kadayıfı. Let them soak for ten or fifteen minutes, then take them out, and place them tastefully on a dish. Sprinkle a little rosewater over, and serve. If rolls are not handy, slices of bread with the crusts taken off can be used instead.

Saray Lokması

A KIND OF DOUGH-NUT, CALLED "PALACE MORSEL"

Ingredients

1lb flour
20 eggs
2 lbs butter
1 1/2 lbs sugar
2 pint of water
1-2 drops cochineal or red food colouring
1-2 drops essence of orange flower or rose

Pound in a mortar half a pound of plain white biscuit, and sift it through a fine sieve. Then beat up the whites of the eggs in a basin, add by degrees the powdered biscuit, and beat it up together until it forms a smooth consistency. Take it up a dessert spoon at a time, pour it into boiling fresh butter, one after the other, any fry them a nice delicate brown. They should be round, and swell up to the size of a peach. When done, drain and place them in a stew pan, half full of boiling water, and let them boil for ten minutes or so; then take it off, and strain the water from them. Then dissolve the sugar in as much water as will cover them, add cochineal, with essence of orange-flower or rose, stir it well, and pour it over them, set the pan on a charcoal fire with the cover over, and let it boil until the syrup is nearly absorbed. Then dish up, and serve hot or cold. Great care must be taken in beating up the eggs well with the powdered biscuit, or it will burst when frying.

Yumurta Lokması

THE SAME, PREPARED WITH EGGS

Ingredients

1 lb flour
1 ts salt
20 Eggs
2 lb butter
1 1/2 lb sugar
2 pint of water
1-2 drops cochineal or red food colouring
1-2 drops essence of orange flower or rose

Put a pound of flour in a stew pan, with a small teaspoon of salt, which mix with water to form a smooth batter.

Set it on a charcoal fire and stir it until it becomes thick, and then take it off. When cold, beat it up with eggs until it becomes a smooth thick batter; then proceed exactly as Saray Lokması; Dish up, and serve with cream over, if approved of.

Gaziler Helvası

THE SWEET OF THE WAR VETERANS

Ingredients

1 1/2 lb flour
1 lb butter
2 pints syrup (See p.123)
1 pint milk
Sugar

Put butter in a very clean stew pan, put it on a charcoal fire, scald it, then take it off. When it gets a little cold, add by degrees the flour, set it again on the fire, and keep stirring until the flour becomes a gold colour, then take it off. Immediately pour boiling syrup over, which you have previously prepared of honey sugar and water as in Tel Kadayıf (see p.131), and a pint of boiling milk.

Put the cover over, and let it remain for five minutes or so; then stir it well with a wooden fork; dish up in tablespoons, and let it bear the impression of the spoon; shake some white sugar over, and serve.

Sabuniye Helvası
SOAPANACIOUS SWEET

Ingredients

1 lb butter
1 lb sugar
1/2 lbs wheat starch
1 pint of water

Put butter in a stew pan, with sugar, pre-viously dissolved in a small quantity of water, and set it on a charcoal fire. When boiling, add by degrees half a pound of wheat-starch, which you have previously made a batter with a pint of water, and keep stirring, tasting it now and then. When it does not stick to the teeth, it is done, then dish up, and serve.

Sabuniye Helvası II
SOAPANACIOUS SWEET II

Ingredients

1/2 lb wheat starch
7 pints water
2 3/4 lb sugar
3/4 lb almonds

Put wheat-starch in a basin, with 6 pints of water, stir it until smooth, and pass it through a fine sieve; then put in a stew pan two pounds and three quarters of sugar, with half a pint of water, and stir until the sugar is dissolved.

Then add by degrees the starch and water, set it on the fire, and stir it gently until it gets very thick. Then add one tablespoon at a time, skinned almonds, and keep stirring. Taste it now and then.

When it does not stick to the teeth pour it into a convenient dish, and, when cold, cut it up in diamonds, dish up, and serve.

Reşidiye Helvası

THE SWEET OF RESHID

Ingredients

1/2 lb butter
1/2 lb wheat starch
1 1/2 pint of water
1 lb sugar
1 tbls rose water
Cinnamon

Put on the fire a stew pan with fresh butter, when it is melted, take it off; then add wheat-starch, which you have previously dissolved in a pint of water, and sugar, previously melted in a little water, set it on the fire, and keep stirring it. When it becomes crummy, stir it a few minutes longer, then take it off, dish up, sprinkle a little rosewater over, with a little powdered cinnamon, and serve.

Asude Helvası

THE SWEET OF PEACE

Ingredients

1 lb wheat starch
1 pint of water
1 lb honey
1/2 lb butter

Put in a clean stew pan wheat-starch, water, honey, and melted fresh butter. Put it on the fire, and commence stirring until the butter begins to appear on the surface of the mixture, which indicates that it is done. Keep stirring from the bottom of the pan, and pressing it with the back of the spoon for a few minutes longer, then dish up like a dome, and serve.

Helva-i Hakani

THE IMPERIAL SWEET

Ingredients

1/2 lb flour
1/2 lb wheat starch
1/2 lb rice flour

Put fresh butter in a stew pan, set it on a charcoal fire. When melted, add by degrees wheat and rice flours and wheat starch, and keep stirring until it becomes a gold

1/2 lb butter
3 pints syrup (see p.123)
2 pints milk

colour. Then pour all at once boiling syrup over, which you have previously prepared of sugar and water, as in Ekmek Kadayıfı (see p.136), and boiling milk; instantly put the cover on the pan, and let it remain for fifteen minutes. Then bruise it with the back of a spoon, dish up a tablespoon at a time, letting it bear the impression of the spoon, and serve.

Helva-i Hakani II

THE IMPERIAL SWEET II

Ingredients

1 3/8 lb
1/4 lb flour
1/4 lb rice flour
1/4 lb wheat starch
3/8 lb almonds
2 1/2 pints syrup
1 1/2 pint milk
3 tbls rosewater
2 pinches cinnamon

Set on a charcoal fire a stew pan with fresh butter: when melted, add flour, rice-flour, and wheat-starch, and keep stirring until the flour becomes a gold colour. Then add six ounces of skinned almonds, and stir for a few minutes longer. Then pour two pints and a half of boiling syrup over, as above, with a pint and a half of boiling milk, instantly put the cover over the pan, and let it remain for fifteen minutes. Then stir it well, dish up, sprinkle some rosewater over, with a little powdered cinnamon, and serve.

Pirinç Unu Helvası

SWEET MADE OF GROUND RICE

Ingredients

1 lb butter
1 1/2 lb rice flour
1/4 lb almonds
1 1/2 pint syrup (see p. 123)

Put in a stew pan fresh butter, and scald it, then remove it from the fire. When a little cold, add by degrees rice-flour, set it again on the fire, and keep stirring for twenty-five minutes, or until the butter appears on the surface of the flour, and the flour swells up

1 1/2 pint milk
3 tbls powdered sugar

like grains of gum powder, which you will easily perceive by taking a little out on the back of the spoon. Then add skinned almonds, and stir it for a few minutes longer; then immediately add a pint and a half of boiling syrup, previously prepared of sugar and water, as in Ekmek Kadayıfı (see p.136), and boiling milk, instantly put the cover over. Let it remain for about five minutes, then stir it well with a wooden fork, dish it up in spoonfuls, and let it bear the impression of the spoon, sprinkle a little powdered sugar over, and serve.

Gülabiyye

SWEET PREPARED WITH ROSEWATER AND MUSK

Ingredients

1 lb sugar
2 pint of water
1/2 lb butter
1 lb wheat starch
1/4 lb almonds
4 tbls rosewater
2 pinches musk

Put sugar in a stew pan, with 1 pint of water, and set it on the fire: when boiling, add butter, wheat-starch, previously formed into a thin batter with water, skinned almonds, and rosewater, mixed with a little musk, and stir it gently until it becomes crummy. Then spread it in a rather deep dish, press it all over with the back of the spoon, cut it up in diamonds, and serve with a little sugar sifted over.

İshakiyye

ISAAC'S SWEET

Ingredients

1 1/2 lb rice flour
1 lb butter

Put on the fire a stew pan butter: when melted, add rice-flour, with almonds, skinned and well pounded, and keep stirring until

3/4 lb almonds
1 pint milk
2 pint syrup (see p..123
3 tbls powdered sugar

it becomes a gold colour. Then immediately addboiling milk, with, boiling syrup that you have previously prepared of sugar and water, as in Ekmek Kadayıfı (see p.136), instantly put the cover over. Let it remain for five minutes, then stir it well with a fork, dish it up in moulds the size of a small teacup, letting it bear the impression of the mould, and serve with some powdered sugar sifted over.

İrmik Helvası

SWEET MADE OF SAGO

Ingredients

1 3/8 lb sago
3/4 lb butter
1/4 lb almonds
1 1/2 milk
1 1/2 syrup (see p.123)
3 tbls powdered sugar
1 tbls Rosewater

Set on the fire a stew pan with fresh butter. When hot, add sago,(1) with skinned almonds, and keep stirring it until the almonds are a nice brown. Then pour in all at once boiling milk, with boiling syrup. Stir it well, put the cover over, and let it remain for fifteen minutes.
Then sprinkle a little rosewater over, dish up, shake some sugar over, and serve.

1) In Turkey the sago is made of plain paste in grains as small as gunpowder.

Hurma

SWEET MADE IN THE SHAPE OF A DATE (FRUIT)

Ingredients

1 1/4 lb flour
1 lb butter
1/2 pint of water

Put flour on the pastry-slab, make a hole in the centre, in which put salt and 1/4 lb of melted butter. Mix, then add water, mixed with a little carbonate of soda, and form it a softly flexible paste.

1 ts carbonate of soda
1 ts salt
Syrup (see p.123)

Then roll it with hands as long as it will extend, a little thicker than your thumb, and cut it up in pieces the size of a date (3/2 inches). Then roll them one by one upon a basket-lid, or a tablemat made of fine twigs, and fry them a delicate colour in boiling fresh butter. When done, let them drain, then throw them in boiling syrup, which you have previously prepared of honey, or sugar and water, as described in the preceding receipts, and let them remain for a few minutes, then dish them up tastefully, and serve.

Vişne Ekmeği
FRUIT CRUSTS

Ingredients

2 lb cherries
2 French penny rolls
2 eggs
8 tbls milk
1/2 lb butter
1 lb sugar
1 pint of water

Put sugar into a stew pan with a pint of water, put it on the fire. When boiling, skim it, and then add two pounds of cherries with the stalks taken off and the stones taken out. Stir with a wooden spoon, and boil them until getting tender.

Then cut two French penny rolls lengthwise in eight slices, put the yolks of the eggs in a basin with milk, and beat it up well.

Dip quickly each slice in it, and fry it a nice colour on both sides in hot fresh butter. When all done, lay them in a convenient pie-dish, them put the cherries over with the syrup. If you find the syrup too thick, add a little water, set it on a moderate charcoal fire, and let it simmer until the syrup is absorbed, then serve.

Vişne Ekmeği II

FRUIT CRUSTS II

Ingredients

2 lb cherries
2 French penny rolls
3 tbls powdered sugar
1 lb sugar
1 pint of water

Prepare some cherries as above; then cut two round penny loaves in slices, and toast them. Then lay them in a pie-dish or saucepan, put the cherries over with the syrup, and nearly cover them with water. Put the pan on the fire, and let it simmer till the slices of toasted bread are soft, then dish up one over the other, laying between them cherries, and sprinkling at the same time powdered sugar over; then serve hot or cold. Apricots, and all kinds of plums, may be done in the same way.

Cızlama

A SWEET DISH, CRUMPETS AND CLOTTED CREAM

Ingredients

1 lb flour
1/2 ts salt
1 ts yeast
1/2 lb clotted cream
1 cup powdered sugar
3/4 lb sugar
1 pint of water
3 tbls butter
2 tbls rose water
Water

Put in a basin or pan the flour, salt, and a very small piece of yeast, which mix with water to form a nice crumpet dough, and keep it covered in a warm place until it has nicely risen. Then pour a portion of it on a stove sufficient to bake a crumpet the size of a dinner plate, and as thick as a crown-piece. When you have baked five or six, lay them in a rather deep and circular baking-tin, one over the other, and between each one a thin layer of clotted cream and powdered sugar over.

Then dissolve in a saucepan sugar with water, add butter, set it on the fire, and commence stirring until the butter is melted. Then pour it over the crumpets, and put the baking-tin on a very slow charcoal fire, or in the oven, for ten or fifteen minutes, then dish it up carefully, sprinkle a little rose water over, and serve.

PART XII.

SOĞUK TATLILAR
COLD SWEET DISHES

Kazan Dibi (Tavuk Göğsü) /Rice Cream, with the Breast of Fowl

Saray Aşuresi /A Kind of Sweet Dish Made of Wheat

Tavuk Göğsü

RICE CREAM, WITH THE BREAST OF FOWL

Ingredients

2 chickens
5 1/2 pints milk
3/4 lb rice flour
3/4 lb powdered sugar
2 tbls rosewater
3 tbls almond oil
2 pinches cinnamon

Boil the chickens: when done, cut off the breasts, remove the bones and the skins from them, and pound the meat in a stone mortar, or pull it in bits like fine threads.

Then pour in a stew pan the milk and put it on the fire.

While boiling, put in a basin the rice flour, which mix with some of the boiling milk and some water, to form a batter. Then add this to the milk and boil it until it becomes a smooth substance, but not too thick.

Then add the pounded breasts of chickens with powdered sugar, and rosewater, and keep stirring, and at the same time beating it up on a slow fire until it forms a rather thick glutinous substance. Then remove it from the fire, stir it for a few minutes longer, then fill a mould previously oiled with almond oil, and place it in cool place.

When ready, dip the mould into warm water, and turn it out on to a dish, sprinkle a little cinnamon over, and serve.

Do not neglect to rinse the pounded breasts of the chickens once or twice in cold water before you add them to the milk ground rice, or it will smell of the fowl.

If cooked with care, it is an enticing and strengthening dish.

Saray Aşuresi

A KIND OF SWEET DISH MADE OF WHEAT

Ingredients

1 lb wheat
3 tbls currants
1/2 pint syrup (see p.123)
2 tbls rose water
2 pinches musk
1 tbls pistachios
1 tbls almonds

Put in a stew pan as much skinned wheat as is required, with plenty of water, set it on the fire, and boil until the grains begin to crack. Then take out with a wooden spoon what pulp there is on the top, and put it in a basin, add some more water, and continue so until you have extracted all the goodness from the grains.

Then strain the remaining grains through a sieve, and put all the pulp you have collected into a saucepan, add washed currants, and syrup.

Put it on a charcoal fire and begin stirring it. When boiling, add musk mixed with rosewater, and stir it one or two minutes longer; then take it off and pour it into a dish arrange on the top tastefully some skinned almonds and pistachios, and serve when cold.

Limon Elmasiyesi

LEMON JELLY

Ingredients

5 lemons
1/2 lb sugar
1 ounces isinglass
1 pint of water
2 tbls rosewater

Dissolve the isinglass in a small tumbler of water, boil and reduce it to half, then pass it through a cloth into a basin; then cut in two the lemons, take off the rind of one of them and remove the pith, place them in a basin, and squeeze the juice of the lemons into it. Then put sugar in a stew pan with a pint of water, set it to boil until it becomes syrup, then take it off and add the juice and the rind of the lemons, put the stew pan again on thefire with the cover over.

As soon as it begins to boil, skim it well assist its clarification. Let it boil one or two minutes longer, then add the isinglass, pass it through a jelly-bag, if fancied, add two tablespoons of rosewater, then pour it into a mould, and place it on ice. When ready, dip the mould in warm water and turn it out.

If summer, add a little more isinglass.

Lamunya Kaymağı

A KIND OF CREAM

Ingredients

- *1 lb strawberries or raspberries*
- *4 tbls powdered sugar*
- *3 tbls water*
- *6 ounces isinglass*
- *1 pint whipped cream*
- *2 drops of essence of rose or orange-flower*

Take off the stalks of strawberries or raspberries, wash and put them in a stew pan, with powdered sugar, and water, put the pan on a moderate charcoal fire, and boil till rather thick, stirring it at the same time with a wooden spoon.

When cold, pass it through a sieve into a basin, add an ounce and a half of melted isinglass to half a pint of the fruit, and stir it well. Then add whipped cream, with essence of rose or orange-flower.

Mix, then pour it into a mould, and place it on ice, or in a cool place, until firm. When ready, turn it out as above, and serve.

Elmasiye / Jelly

Portakal Elmasiyesi

ORANGE JELLY

Ingredients

6 oranges
5 tbls powdered sugar
1 pint of water
1 ounces isinglass
2 drops of cochineal or red food colouring

Take off the rind of one of the oranges , and remove the pith, place them in a basin. Squeeze the juice of the other oranges in it, then put powdered sugar in a saucepan with 1/2 pint of water, and boil it until it becomes syrup.

Then take it off, and add the juice and the rind of the oranges. Put the saucepan again on the fire with the cover over. As soon as it begins to boil, skim it well, and add gradually a small teacup of water.

Let it boil one or two minutes longer, then add an ounce of isinglass, dissolved as directed in Limon Elmasiyesi.

Stir well, and pass it through a jelly-bag until clear.

Then add cochineal, and pour it in a mould. Place it on ice until firm, then turn it out as before, and serve.

If the oranges are very sweet, add less; and if summer, add a little more isinglass.

İncik Elmasiyesi

CALF'S FOOT JELLY

Ingredients

4 calf's feet
7 3/4 pints of water
1 1/2 lb sugar
4 lemons
5 eggs
1-2 drops essence of rose or orange-flower
10-12 grapes
10-12 cherries
10-12 strawberries

Procure the calf's feet, wash and place them in a stew-pan, with 6 pints of water, and put it on the fire. When boiling, skim and simmer until the flesh comes off the bones; then pass it through a clean cloth or a sieve into a basin, and let it remain until quite hard, then remove all the fat, etc..., from the top.

Then put in a saucepan sugar, 1 3/4 pints of water, the juice of the lemons, and the rind of one, with the pith taken off, the whites and shells of the eggs, and stir with a wooden spoon until the sugar is dissolved.

Then add the jelly, set it on the fire, and stir well until it boils. Then pass it through a jelly bag until quite clear, add the essence of rose or orange-flower, and then put it in a mould, with grapes, strawberries and cherries. Place it on ice until quite firm, turn it out as above, and serve.

Zübde-i Hünkâri
IMPERIAL CREAM

Ingredients

3 small glasses maraschino
1 1/2 ounce isinglass (melted)
1 pint of whipped cream
6 tbls powdered sugar
3/4 teacup rosewater
2 pinches musk

Put in basin powdered sugar, rosewater, mixed with a little musk, maraschino, an ounce and a half of melted isinglass.

Stir it well, and then add a pint of whipped cream.

Stir it again three or four times, put it in a mould, and set it on ice until firm; turn it out as before, and serve.

Muhallebi
A KIND OF RICE CREAM

Ingredients

3 pints milk
7 ounces rice flour
4 ounces powdered sugar
1-2 drops of the essence of orange-flower
3 tbls almond oil

Pour into a stew pan milk, set it on the fire, as soon as it commences to boil, put rice-flour in a basin, which mix with milk or water, to form a smooth batter.

Then add it to milk, with three or four ounces of powdered sugar and essence of orange-flower, and keep stirring it until it forms a smooth substance, but not too thick. Then pour it into a mould previously oiled with almond oil.

Put it on ice, or in cold water, and, when firm, dip the mould in warm water, turn it out on to a dish, ornament the top with pieces of clotted cream, the size of nuts, and serve.

Güllaç Baklavası

A KIND OF DELICATE CONFECTION PREPARED WITH ROSEWATER

Ingredients

20 eggs
1 lb wheat starch
1/2 lb butter (melted)
2 tbls rosewater
2 cups milk
1 lb clotted cream
1 lb sugar
2 pints water

Put in a basin the whites of the eggs, and whip them up well, then add wheat starch by degrees, stir it well, and mix it well with water, to form a very thin batter. Then put over a charcoal fire a circular and slightly domed sheet-iron, the under side in the center of which you have previously cemented with ashes half an inch thick, to prevent it from getting fiercely hot. When moderately hot, pour a portion of the butter over the center, with a convenient spoon, sufficient to form a round cake, the size of a large dinner-plate, or larger, and which will be done in less than a minute: it ought to be very white, and as thin as tissue-paper. When you have prepared fifty or sixty pieces in this manner, lay half of them in a suitable baking-tin, one over the other, sprinkling between each piece some rosewater and milk as you lay them. Then lay some clotted cream over; then cover it with the other half of take cakes, sprinkling rosewater and milk between each one as before. Then put in a stew pan sugar, with water, and set it to boil until it becomes syrup. Then take it off and pour it over the cakes, until covered, and let it remain covered until cold. Then cut it up in diamonds, dish up and serve. Pounded almond or pistachios may be used, if clotted cream is not handy.

These cakes are sold ready made in Istanbul, and they can be obtained through any Turkish merchant residing in this country. It is a delicate and most delicious dish when properly done.

Güllaç Kızartması

ANOTHER SORT, FRIED IN FRESH BUTTER

Ingredients

30 sheet of güllaç (see p..155)
1 teacup rosewater
6 tbls almonds or pistachios
4 eggs
1 lb butter
Syrup (see p..123)

Prepare twenty or thirty cakes as Güllaç Baklavası (see p.155) and moisten them by sprinkling rosewater over, then fold them in two separately, put on each one some pounded almonds or pistachios.

Then fold them in square or triangular shape, dip them in egg, and fry them a delicate colour on both sides in hot fresh butter. Drain them, and then throw them in boiling syrup, prepared as above.

When sufficiently soaked, take them out with a spoon, arrange them tastefully on a dish, and serve hot or cold.

Güllaç Paludesi

THE SAME, PREPARED LIKE JELLY

Ingredients

30 sheets of güllaç (see p. 155)
1 lb sugar
2 pints water
1 teacup rose water
3 tbls almonds or pistachios

Put a sugar in a stew pan, with water, and set it to boil until it becomes syrup. Then take it off, and pour it into a rather deep baking-tin, and put it on a moderate charcoal fire. When boiling put in a cake (Güllaç Baklavası see p.155) and bruise it with the back of a wooden spoon, and continue in this manner as many cakes as it will take.

When thick, take it off, sprinkle some rosewater over, and let it remain until cold; then dish it up, ornament the top with some skinned almonds or pistachios, and serve.

Sütlü aş (Sütlaç) / Rice Pudding

Sütlü Aş (Sütlaç)
RICE PUDDING

Malzeme

1 cup rice
2 3/4 pint milk
1 cup powdered sugar

Wash and scald the rice, and drain it; then pour into a stew pan of the milk and set it on the fire. As soon as it commences to boil, add the rice, and let it simmer until quite soft. Then take it off and pour it into a pie-dish; then put it on a very slow charcoal fire, covered with ashes, or on the hob, and let it remain for about fifteen minutes, during which time the top of the rice will be covered with cream. When cold, sprinkle powdered sugar over, and serve. You may sweeten the rice while boiling, and add one or two tablespoons of rosewater.

Nazlı Aş

FASCINATING PUDDING

Ingredients

1/2 lb rice
3 pints water
5 tbls wheat starch
2 drops of the essence of rose or orange-flower
2 tbls almond oil
6 tbls pistachios or almonds

Pound, rather coarse, the rice in a mortar; then put three pints of water in a stew pan, then add the wheat starch and pounded rice, and stir it well. When as smooth as milk, put it on a moderate charcoal fire, and continually stir it for about three hours, or until it forms a smooth substance, but not too thick. Then add essence of rose or orange-flower, stir it for a few minutes longer, and then pour it into a mould previously oiled with almond-oil. Put it on ice, or in a cool place, till firm. When ready, dip the mould in warm water and turn it out, and serve. It is a light and pleasant dish. You can ornament the top with some skinned pistachios or almonds.

Palude

A KIND OF JELLY

Ingredients

2 lb sugar
5 tbls wheat strach
2 quarts water
2 tbls almond oil
1-2 drops essence of rose or orange

Dissolve two pounds of sugar in a stewpan, with two quarts of water; then add about five ounces of wheat starch, and stir it well. When as smooth as milk, put it on a moderate charcoal fire, and continually stir it for about three hours, or until it forms a smooth substance, but not too thick; then add a few drops of the essence of rose or orange-flower, stir it for a few minutes longer, and then pour it into a mould previously oiled with almond-oil; put it on ice, or in a cool place, till firm. When ready, dip the mould in warm water and turn it out, and serve. İt is a light and pleasant dish. You can ornament the top with some skinned pistachios or almonds.

Lokum
TURKISH DELIGHT

Ingredients

1 lb wheat starch
3 1/2 lb sugar
4 quarts water
1/4 pint rose water
3 pinches musk
5 tbls almond oil

The comfort of the throat (it is commonly known in England as the "Lumps or morsels of delight")

Put 2 3/4 lb sugar in a very clean stew pan, with water, and stir with a wooden spoon until the sugar is dissolved. Then set it on a moderate charcoal fire, and immediately add 8 1/2 ounces wheat starch by degrees, stirring it at the same time so as to prevent it from getting lumpy and continue stirring it from the bottom of the pan until it forms a smooth substance, then take a little out, and let drop a few drops on powdered sugar. If it moistens or absorbs the sugar it is not done, and if it does not it is done.

Then mix a little musk, in rosewater, and add this to it; stir it for half a minute or a minute longer. Then take it off and pour it into a convenient dish or a plated pan about an inch deep, which you have previously oiled with almond-oil. When cold, cut it in pieces an inch broad and two long, and dip them in sifted sugar mixed with half the quantity of fine wheat starch. See that they are well covered, to prevent them from sticking to each other, and serve as a dessert.

This celebrated a delicious confection may be kept for a long time in a wooden box, such as a fig-box.

Badem Kurabiyesi / Almond Cakes

Badem Kurabiyesi
ALMOND CAKES

Ingredients

2 3/4 lb almonds
2 3/4 lb sugar
4 eggs
1 tbls gum mastic
23 pinches cinnamon

Put skinned almonds in a stone mortar, with sugar, and pound them together until very fine; then add the egg whites, powdered mastic, and cinnamon, and pound them for a few minutes longer.

When like a paste, make it into small cakes the size of macaroons, or any size and shape you place. Then lay on the bottom of a baking-tin some paper, and arrange the cakes over. Then cover them with paper, turn up the edges of the papers that are on the bottom of the tin and fix them to the top ones, to prevent the cakes from burning.

Bake for about an hour in a rather hot oven. Sometimes a little musk mixed with rosewater is used instead of the white of egg, and sometimes a little lemon-peel and a little cochineal is added.

PART XIII.

Kayganalar / Omelettes

Kaygana

PLAIN OMELETTES

Ingredients

4 eggs
2 tbls butter
Salt
Pepper

Break the eggs in a basin, add a little salt and pepper, and beat them up with a fork. Then put into a very clean frying-pan fresh butter and put in on the fire. When hot, pour in the eggs, and keep stirring until all is nicely set. Then let it slip to the edge of the pan, laying hold by the handle and raising it slantwise, let it set a moment, then turn it over on to a dish, and serve.

It ought to be a nice yellow colour, done to a nicety, and as light and delicate as possible.

Kıymalı Kaygana

OMELETTES WITH MINCED MEAT

Ingredients

4 eggs
4 tbls mutton
1 onion
1 tbls parsley
5 tbls butter
Salt
Pepper

Mince raw mutton, with an onion and a little parsley, and partly fry them in a little fresh butter.

Then break into a basin the eggs, and beat them up well with a fork; add the minced meat, &c., with half a teaspoon of salt and a pinch or two of pepper, and beat them up well.

Then put four ounces of butter into the frying pan, and put it on the fire.

When hot, pour in the mixture, and fry a delicate colour on both sides, as above. When done, turn it on to a dish carefully, and serve.

Patlıcan Kayganası

OMELETTES WITH EGGPLANTS

Ingredients

6 eggs
1 eggplant
1 tbls currants
2 tbls pine nuts
Pepper
2 pinches cinnamon
4 tbls butter

Peel the eggplant, take out the inside, if seeded, and grate it or chop it up fine. Then scald it in moderately-salt water, strain and squeeze from it all the water in a cloth.

Then break in a basin the eggs, beat them well up, and add the eggplants, with currants, pine nuts, a little pepper and cinnamon, mix well all together, put in the frying-pan four or five ounces of fresh butter, put it on the fire till hot, then pour in the mixture and fry it a nice brown on both sides, as above. When done, turn it over carefully on to a dish, and serve.

The addition of three or four table-spoons of fried minced mutton or beef will improve it.

Tatlı Kaygana

SWEET OMELETTES

Ingredients

4 eggs
1 tbls milk
1/2 tbls sugar
4 tbls butter
1 tbls powdered sugar
Salt

Break five eggs in a basin, and beat them up; add milk, sugar, a little salt, and beat them well up.

Then put three or four ounces of fresh butter in the frying-pan, pour in the eggs, fry a nice colour, as Kaygana, and serve with powdered sugar over.

Maydanozlu Kaygana
OMELETTES WITH HERBS

Ingredients

4 eggs
2 tbls butter
Salt - Pepper
1 tbls parsley (chopped)
1/4 tbls onions

Proceed exactly as Kaygana, add chopped parsley, finely chopped onions, or spring onions, salt and pepper, fry as above, and serve.

Reçelli Kaygana
OMELET WITH PRESERVES

Ingredients

4 eggs
2 tbls jam
2 tbls powdered sugar

Proceed as Kaygana. When the omelette is nearly cooked put in the centre some jam of any sort, turn the edges over, let it set a moment, then turn it over on to a dish, shake some powdered sugar over, and serve.

Çılbır
POACHED EGGS, WITH STEWED ONIONS

Ingredients

6 eggs
4 onions
4 tbls butter
1 pint of water
1 tbls vinegar
Salt

Peel and slice the onions, and fry them a nice brown in fresh butter, lay them on the bottom of a dish, and keep it hot.

Then pour in a pan a pint of water, add a little salt, and vinegar, put it on the fire, when boiling, break carefully in the pan the eggs, simmer till the white is firm, then take them out with a slice, and arrange them over the onions. Then pour a little hot fresh butter over them, sprinkle a little pepper and powdered cinnamon over, and serve while hot.

Hoşmerim / Cream-Cheese

Hoşmerim
CREAM-CHEESE

Ingredients

2 pounds cream cheese
1 tbls flour
1/2 lb powdered sugar or honey

Get very fresh cream-cheese, break it in small pieces into a stew pan, put it on the fire, and stir until it is melted.

Then add the flour, and keep stirring until the butter begins to run from the cheese. Then take it off, dish up, and serve with some powdered sugar or honey over.

PART XIV.

VEGETABLES

The vegetables that are bitter or acid, such as artichokes, dandelion, and sorrel, are first scalded before they are cooked. If large, they are cut in pieces and placed in a stew pan, with a sufficient quantity of water, salt, and a few sliced onions previously fried a nice brown in butter or olive oil.

To those that are cooked with onions fried in butter is added three or four tablespoons of minced mutton or beef, previously fried a delicate brown in butter, or in the fat that comes from them, or half o dozen pieces of mutton or beef the size of walnuts, fried in butter, and some broth, and simmered on a charcoal fire till the liquor is nearly absorbed.

Others, such as leeks, asparagus, celery, and cauliflower, &c., are cooked as above, and dressed with egg-sauce, which is prepared by beating the eggs up with lemon-juice, and thickened on a slow fire by continually stirring.

Other, such as minced spinach, sorrel, &c., are served with poached eggs over, and fried or toasted bread, cut in diamonds, round the dish. Others, such as eggplants or aubergines, vegetable marrow, &c., are peeled and cut in slices crosswise or lengthwise, then the slices dipped first in flour, and then in egg, and fried in butter.

In some of the vegetables, tomato-juice is used instead of broth. In Turkey, vegetables are never cooked in simple water.

Fasulye Piyazı / Bean Salad

PART XV.

SALATALAR / SALADS

Tarator

Hıyar Taratoru

CUCUMBER SALAD

Ingredients

2 cucumbers
1 lb almonds or nuts
4 cloves of garlic
1/2 French penny roll
1/2 teacup wine vinegar or 3 lemons
Salt
White pepper
2 tbs olive oil

Crack the nuts or almonds, scald and skin them, then pound them in a stone mortar; add half a teaspoonful of salt, the garlic cloves peeled, and pound them well together with the nuts. Then add the crumb of the French penny roll, previously soaked in water, and pound again all together until it forms a smooth substance like paste. Then moisten it with vinegar, or the juice of three lemons, and bring it to the consistency of cream with some water, stirring it all the time with a wooden spoon.

Then peel and cut in thin slices the cucumbers in a dish, season with a little salt and white pepper, and pour the sauce over. Then pour the olive oil over by degrees, and serve.

The leaves of parsley make a nice salad with the above sauce. Broccoli, cauliflower, and the stalks of spinach, previously scalded; also make o good salad with the same sauce.

Sardalye Salatası

SARDINE SALAD

Ingredients

1 lb Sardines
1 bunch of parsley (chopped)
1 onion (chopped)
1 pint vinegar

Put the sardines in a basin, with the 1 glass of vinegar, and let them remain in it for half an hour, then scrape off the scales gently, wash them in fresh vinegar, and arrange them round the edge of a dish. Then put in the centre of it chopped parsley, onions, and the olives, all mixed.

24 olives
1/2 teacup olive oil
2 lemons
Salt

Then put half a teaspoon of salt in a basin, with two or three tablespoonfuls of the best wine vinegar, or the juice of two lemons, and the olive oil, and beat up well with a wooden fork or spoon until it becomes like cream, then pour it over the sardines and the parsley, and serve.

Balık Yumurtası Taratoru

FISHEGG SALAD

Ingredients

1 lb fish egg
1 teacup olive oil
2 lemons
2 tbls pine nuts or almonds

Pound the fish eggs well in a stone mortar, then add a teaspoon of the best olive oil, the same of lemon-juice, an pound it again; add another teaspoon of oil and lemon-juice, and beat it up well, and continue in this way until you bring it to the consistency of a very thick cream. Then pour it in a dish or plate, ornament the top with some skinned pistachios or almonds, and serve. In Turkey, it is served at breakfast and at luncheon, as in the middle of the dinner, to sharpen the appetite.

Uskumru Balığı Taratoru

MACKEREL SALAD

Ingredients

4 mackerel
1/2 ts cayenne pepper
Cucumber salad (see p. 171)

Clean and boil the mackerels. When cold, remove the heads and extract all the bones, arrange the fish in a dish, and dress it as Hıyar Taratoru, sprinkle a little cayenne pepper over, and serve.

Remains of cold turbot, cot, soles, brill, plaice, and sturgeon, either boiled or fried, may all be dressed in the same way.

Cacık

CUCUMBER SALAD, WITH YOGHURT

Ingredients

2 small cucumbers
3 cloves of garlic
2 pint yoghurt

Peel and cut in thin small dice the cucumbers, sprinkle them with sufficient salt, and toss them up. Then pound the garlic cloves, and put them in a bowl, add the yoghurt and beat it up with water until you bring it to the thickness of thin cream. Then put the cucumbers in, with a few pieces of ice, stir it, and serve.

This is generally served at the end or the middle of the dinner, and it is very refreshing in summer.

Cacık II

CUCUMBER SALAD, WITH YOGHURT II

Ingredients

2 cucumbers
2 cloves of garlic
3 tbls wine vinegar
1 tbls water
2 tbls olive oil
1/2 bunch of parsley (chopped)
Salt

Peel and cut in four lengthwise the cucumbers, and them cut them in thin slices, sprinkle a little salt over, and shake them up. Then pound the garlic cloves in a stone mortar, add the vinegar, water, olive oil and stir it well.

Then arrange the slices of cucumber in a plate with a handful of chopped parsley, and pour the vinegar and oil over, and serve.

Teke Salatası

PRAWN SALAD

Ingredients

1 lb prawns
1/2 bunch of parsley (picked)
2 lemons
3 tbls olive oil
Salt

Take off the skins and the heads of the prawns, arrange them in a dish with parsley, sprinkle a pinch or two of salt over, with the juice of the lemons, and the oil, and serve.

Marul Salatası

COS LETTUCE SALAD

Ingredients

3 lettuces
2 eggs
1 1/2 tbls wine vinegar
3 tbls olive oil
1/4 bunch of chervil (chopped)
1 ts tarragon
1 spring onion (chopped)
1 small beetroot (sliced)
Salt
Pepper

Remove the faded and all the coarse green leaves of the lettuces, and cut the green top off. Then pull the leaves off one by one, and cut them in three or four pieces, according to the size of each leaf; well wash and drain them in a cloth. Then put in a salad-bowl half a teaspoon of salt, one or two pinches of pepper, the hard boiled egg yolks, then bruise them to a pulp with the back of a wooden spoon.

Then add half a tablespoon of wine vinegar or lemon-juice, stir it round, pour a tablespoon of olive oil over by degrees, and keep stirring. Add a spoonful more of vinegar, and two of oil, and beat them well up.

When as smooth as cream, add the lettuce, chervil, tarragon, spring onion, and the beetroot slices. Turn the salad gently till well mixed and serve.

Top Marul Salatası
CABBAGE LETTUCE SALAD

Ingredients

2 cabbage-lettuces
1 small beetroot (sliced)
2 eggs
1/4 bunch of chervil (chopped)
1 ts tarragon
1 spring onion (chopped)
3 tbls olive oil
1 1/2 tbls vinegar
Salt
Pepper

Remove the outer leaves of cabbage-lettuces and throw them away, pull the others one by one, then wash and well drain them in a cloth. Put them in the bowl, with a few slices of beetroot, hard-boiled eggs cut in quarters, chervil, tarragon and spring onion.

Sprinkle over with your fingers half a teaspoon of salt, one or two pinches of pepper, the olive oil, and vinegar, or the juice of a lemon.

Turn the salad in the bowl with a spoon and fork until well mixed, and serve.

Frenk Teresi Salatası
NASTURTIUM SALAD

Ingredients

1/2 lb Nasturtium
1/4 bunch of chervil (chopped)
3 tbls olive oil
1 lemon
Salt

Put a plate of flowers of the nasturtium in a salad-bowl, with chervil. Sprinkle over with your fingers half a teaspoon of salt, two or three tablespoons of olive oil, and the juice of a lemon.

Turn the salad in the bowl with a spoon and fork until well mixed, and serve.

Hindiba Salatası
ENDIVE SALAD

Ingredients

3 heads of endive
1 lemon
3 tbls olive oil
Salt
Pepper

Remove the dark green leaves of endive, pick off the others one by one, and cut the large ones in two. Wash and drain them in a cloth by shaking violently, and extract all the water.

Then put in the salad-bowl a small teaspoon of salt, one or two pinches of pepper, the juice of a lemon, three tablespoons of olive oil, and beat up until it becomes like cream, then put in the salad, and turn it with spoon and fork till well mixed, and serve.

A tablespoon of chopped chervil and one of chives is a great improvement.

Dandelion may be dressed in the same way.

PART XVI.

TURŞULAR / PICKLES

Karşık Turşu / Mixed Pickled Vegetable

Patlıcan Turşusu
PICKLED EGGPLANTS

Ingredients

8 eggplants
1 bunch of parsley
1 stalks of celery
12 cloves of garlic

Take the stalks off the eggplants, split each one in three or four lengthwise, without separating from the bottom, and scald them. Then place them in a wicker-basket one over the other, put a piece of board or a plate over them, over which place an iron weight, and let them remain for eight or ten hours, so as to draw the bitter juice from them. Then chop up some parsley and celery, which mix with garlic cloves, each cut in two. Then stuff between each slice of the eggplants with the ingredients, and tie up each slice of the eggplants with the stalks of celery, to prevent the stuffing from falling out. Then arrange them in a stone jar one over the other, cover them with wine vinegar, place a piece of clean board over, and on the top an iron weight to press it. Let it remain for about three weeks. It is then ready for use.

Hıyar Turşusu
PICKLED CUCUMBER

Ingredients

2 lb small cucumbers
1 bunch of fennel
Salted water

Put some fennel on the bottom of a stone jar, and place the cucumbers over; lay some fennel on the top, and cover them with salt water; then place a piece of board over them, and on the top an iron weight or a heavy stone, to press it. Put the jar for a few days in a place where the sun is powerful, or in a warm place, then remove it to a cool place, and let it remain eight or ten days before using.

Vegetable marrow may be done in the same way.

Karışık Turşu
MIXED PICKLED VEGETABLES

Ingredients

12 gherkins
12 vegetable marrows (finger sized)
12 melons (walnut sized)
12 water melons (walnut sized)
12 pumpkins (walnut sized)
18 button onions
Wine vinegar

Procure gherkins, vegetable marrows, melons, water-melons, pumpkins, and button onions.

Then scald and drain them, prick each one here and there with a wooden needle, arrange them in a stone jar, cover them with wine vinegar, and let it remain covered for ten or fifteen days before using.

If it is to be kept for any length of time, change the vinegar every five days.

Çağla Turşusu
PICKLED UNRIPE FRUITS

Ingredients

1 lb unripe fruits
Wine vinegar

Gather any unripe fruit that may have fallen from the trees, such as peaches, nectarines, almonds, apricots, cherries, apples, plums, pears, &c.; mix all together, and place them in bottles or in a stone jar, cover them with very strong wine vinegar, tie up the mouths of the bottles with a piece of leather, and let them remain for thirty or forty days before using.

Lahana Turşusu

PICKLED CABBAGE

Ingredients

3 white-heart cabbages
1 ts yeast
6 capsicums
Brine

Cut the stalks off, remove the outer leaves of the white-heart cabbages, and cut them in four crosswise; then put a little yeast on the bottom of a convenient stone jar, place the cabbages over, add ripe capsicums, chopped fine, cover them with brine, put the lid over the jar, and place it in the pantry.

Pour the brine in the jar to and fro every five days. When the cabbage is turned acid, it is then fit for use.

Biber Turşusu

PICKLED GREEN CAPSICUMS

Ingredients

1 lb capsicums
1 bunch of parsley
1 bunch mint
Wine vinegar

Cut the stalks off the capsicums, and scald them. Then place them in a wicker basket, place a piece of clean board or a plate over them, and on the top an iron weight, and let it remain for one night, so as the bitter juice may drain from them.

Then place them in a stone jar, with some parsley and mint between them, and cover them with strong wine vinegar.

Cover the jar, and let it remain in the pantry for ten or fifteen days before using.

If you wish them to be kept for any length of time, change the vinegar occasionally.

Kırmızı Lahana Turşusu
PICKLED RED CABBAGE

Ingredients

3 red cabbages
5 peppercorns
1 bunch of parsley
1/2 bunch mint
1/2 bunch thyme
Salt
Wine vinegar

Cut the red cabbages into thin slices, remove the hard stalks, place them on a dish, or board, and cover them with salt for ten or twelve hours, turn them now and then.

Then clean off all the salt, and lay them in a stone jar with peppercorns, and parsley mixed with mint and thyme. Cover them with strong wine vinegar, put the lid on the jar, and let it remain in a place for three or four weeks before using.

Pancar Turşusu
PICKLED BEET-ROOTS

Ingredients

4 beetroots
2 cloves of garlic
1 tbls sugar
1/2 pint wine vinegar

Cut the stalks off and well wash the beetroots and boil them till tender. Then peel and cut them into rather thin slices, and arrange them in a jar or glass bowl, with half a pint of the water in which they are boiled; then pound cloves of garlic in a stone mortar with a little salt, add an sugar, and half a pint of nice wine vinegar, stir well, and pour it over the beetroots, then ready for use.

Balık Turşusu
PICKLED FISH

Ingredients

6 lb salmon or sword-fish
1 cup olive oil
2 pinches saffron dissolved in 1/2 teacup of water
3 pints wine vinegar
2 tbls sugar
10 cloves of garlic
Bay-leafs
Myrtle leafs
Mixed spice
10-12 peppercorns

Cut the fish in slices three-quarters of an inch thick, wash and dry them well in a cloth, sprinkle them with sufficient salt, and fry them a nice brown in olive oil. Then pour the vinegar in a stew pan with saffron-water, and sugar, stir it round, and partly boil it. Then peel the garlic cloves, and cut them in pieces the size of pine nuts; then lay some bay-leaves and myrtle-leaves on the bottom of a stone jar. Place some of the slices of fish over, sprinkle some mixed spice over them, with some pieces of garlic, washed peppercorns, and skinned pine nuts.

Then lay bay-leaves and myrtle leaves, then fish, then spice, garlic, pine nuts, and peppercorns, &c., until the jar is fully, bay-leaves and myrtle-leaves on the top. Then pour the boiled vinegar until the fish is covered, place a piece of clean board or a plate over, on the top of which put an iron weight, to press it, cover the jar, and let it remain for three days before using. It will keep for some time, and is excellent in summer days with salad or without.

Mackerel, fresh herrings, smelts, and any other kind of fish, if cut in pieces or slices, may be done in the same.

Üzüm Turşusu

PICKLED GRAPES

Ingredients

10 lb white or black grapes
6 tbls mustard seeds

Pick out the best bunches of the grapes and squeeze the juice from the bruised and small ones, pass it through a sieve into a stew pan, free from smell, and set it to boil for a few minutes.

Then wash the bunches you have selected, and lay two or three of them on the bottom of a stone jar; then sprinkle some mustard-seeds over, then grapes, again mustard-seeds over, then grapes, and continue so till the whole of the grapes are laid. Then pour the boiled grape juice over, cover the jar air-tight, and let it remain for thirty or forty days before using.

They will keep for a long time, and are very refreshing because of their agreeable acidity.

Şalgam Turşusu

PICKLED TURNIPS

Ingredients

4 lb turnips
5 tbls mustard-seeds
2 cups sugar
1 quart wine vinegar

Peel and cut in four crosswise the turnips, and boil them in plenty of water till nearly tender.

Then take out the turnips into a colander, put a moderate quantity of powdered mustard seeds in the water, and let it remain for two or three hours.

Then pass it through a cloth or a sieve into a basin, and sweeten it just sufficient to taste the sugar. Then place the turnips in a stone jar, and half cover them with the sweetened water, and half with nice wine vinegar. Put the cover over the jar, and let it remain a few days before using.

Yoğurt

YOGHURT / HOW TO MAKE YOGHURT

Ingredients

4 pints of milk
2 tbls yoghurt

Put pure milk into a particularly clean stew pan, put it on a charcoal fire, let it bubble once; then take it off, and pour it into a basin.

When cold enough to bear your finger in it, add two tablespoons of old yoghurt, and stir it well, with the handle of a wooden spoon.

Put the basin on some straw in a warm corner of the pantry, cover the basin all over with a piece of flannel three or four thickness, and let it remain for ten or twelve hours; you will then find it nicely set, and the top covered with cream, and serve as it is.

In Turkey, this is generally served with the pilaff. It may also be served at breakfast and at luncheon. It is a very refreshing dish on account of its slight and pleasant acidity.

İncir Tatlısı / Stewed Fig

PART XVII.

Meyve Tatlilari
Stewed Fruits

Armut Tatlısı

STEWED PEARS

Ingredients

6 pears
1 pint syrup (see p.123)
4 cloves
2 drops cochineal or red food colouring

Peel and take off the stalks the pears. If too large, cut them in two, and remove the cores. Place them in a stew pan with syrup, as Stewed Peaches, cloves, prepared cochineal, and let it simmer gently on a slow fire until the pears are tender. Then take it off, and serve cold.

Apples may be done the same way; only the cores must be taken out, and, if too large, must be cut in two.

Ayva Tatlısı

STEWED QUINCES

Ingredients

6 quinces
1 pint of syrup (see p.123)
2 drops cochineal or red food colouring
6 cloves

Peel the quinces, remove the cores with a scoop, and ornament the exterior with a sharp instrument. As you finish them, put them in cold water. When all is ready, scald them. Then take them out, and arrange them in another stew pan, pour over the syrup, as Stewed Peaches. Then put the cores with the pips in a small saucepan, with part of the water in which the quinces are boiled.

Put it on the fire until reduced to a pulp, pass it through a sieve, and add it to the fruit with prepared cochineal, and the cloves. Put the pan on the fire, and let it simmer gently until the fruit is tender, and then take it off. When cold, dish it up with the syrup, and serve.

Ingredients

8 peaches
1/2 lb sugar
1 pint of water

Şeftali Tatlısı

STEWED PEACHES

Peel rather unripe peaches, divide each one in two, remove the stones, and the red parts where the stones have been, then arrange them in a stew pan. Put in a saucepan the sugar, with water, and set it to boil until it becomes syrup. Then pour it over the peaches, put the pan on the fire till they are tender. Then place them on a dish tastefully, pour the syrup over, and serve.

Nectarines, greengages, plums of all kinds, and apricots, may all be stewed in the same way.

PART XVIII.

HOŞAF VE ŞERBETLER
SHERBETS, OR THIN SYRUPS WITH FRUIT IN THEM

Vişne Hoşafı
CHERRY HOSHAB

Ingredients

3 lb cherries
1 1/4 lb sugar
2 pint of water
1-2 drops of essence of orange-flower

Procure fresh cherries, pick out the large ones, and squeeze the juice from the small ones through a cloth into a saucepan, add sugar, and boil it for one minute. Put the large ones into a stew pan with water, and set it to boil until the cherries are tender, and then take it off. When partly cold, take the cherries out carefully, without bruising them. Then put in a glass bowl about two pints of the water in which a few drops of the essence of orange-flower or rose, and three or four pieces of ice, and serve.

The reason of boiling the fruit without sugar is to prevent it from sinking when put into the sherbet.

Strawberries, raspberries, red and white currants, and gooseberries, may all be done in the same way. It is a pleasant and refreshing beverage.

Kayısı Hoşafı
APRICOT HOSHAB

Ingredients

3 lb apricots
3 1/2 pint of water
1 1/4 lb sugar
1-2 drops of essence of almonds

Pick out the large apricots, and put the small ones in saucepan, with half a pint of water, or a little more; set it to boil until the stones come out. Then pass them through a cloth into a basin, and well squeeze the juice from them. Put the juice in the pan with sugar; set it to boil for a minute, and pass it again through the cloth into the basin. Then put the large ones in a saucepan, with water, and boil them until they begin to crack, and then take it off.

When cold, pass the liquor through a sieve into a glass bowl. According to taste, sweeten it with the syrup that you have prepared. Then add the apricots, with a few drops of the essence of almonds, or any other essence you fancy, and a few pieces of ice, and serve.

Rızaki Üzümü Hoşafı
RAISIN HOSHAB

Ingredients

1 lb raisins
2 pints water
1 cup sugar

Take off the stalks of the raisins, wash and place them in a stew pan, with two or three pints of water.

Set it to boil until they are quite swollen up. Then, according to palate, add some powdered sugar, and boil them for one or two minutes longer; then take it off.

When cold, pour all together into a glass bowl, add a few drops of any essence of flowers, with some pieces of ice, and serve.

İncir Hoşafı
FIG HOSHAB

Ingredients

2 lb figs
3 pint of water
1-2 drops of orange-flower

Cut off the stalks of the figs, prick each one here and there with a wooden needle, place them in a basin with two or three pints of hot or cold water, and let them remain for ten or twelve hours. Then pass the liquid through a sieve into a glass bowl, and add the figs with a few drops of orange-flower, and a few pieces of ice, and serve.

It is a refreshing and wholesome beverage.

Dried apples may be done in the same way.

Armut Kurusu Hoşafı
DRY PEAR HOSHAB

Ingredients

2 lb dried pears
3 pints of water
3-4 cloves
1 cup sugar

Wash the dried pears; then cut each one in four crosswise, remove the cores, put them in an earthen pan, pour boiling water over, cover the pan, and leave it for one night. Then place them in a stew pan with the liquid, according to palate, add some powdered sugar, with a few cloves, and set it to boil for a few minutes, and then take it off.

When cold, pass the liquid into a glass bowl through a sieve; put in the pears, with a few small pieces of ice, and serve. Dried apples may be done in the same way.

Portakal Hoşafı
ORANGE HOSHAB

Ingredients

8 oranges
4 tbls sugar
1-2 essence of orange-flower

Peel six oranges, and divide them in pieces; cut each clove or piece of orange in two, and remove the pips and the thin membranes from them; then put four ounces sugar in a stew pan, with the juice of two oranges.

If they are not sufficiently sweet, add more sugar. Put it on a slow fire, and stir with a wooden spoon until it begins to boil, and then take it off.

When cold, pour in a glass bowl, and mix it with water to form a nice sherbet; then add the pieces of orange, with a few drops of the essence of orange-flower, and a few small pieces of ice, and serve.

Nar Hoşafı
POMEGRANATE HOSHAB

Ingredients

4 pomegranates
4 tbls sugar

Cut open the pomegranates, take the grains out, pick up the large ones and put the small ones in a cloth, and squeeze all the juice from them into a saucepan.

Add sugar, with the same quantity of water as the juice and stir on a slow fire until it becomes thick; then remove it. When cold, proceed exactly as above.

Antep Fıstığı Hoşafı

PISTACHIO HOSHAB

Ingredients

1 lb pistachios
1 teacup rosewater
1 cup sugar
4 cup water

Skin the pistachios, then pound the broken and part of the small ones very fine in a stone mortar. Then add rosewater, stir it well, and pass it through a clean cloth into a glass bowl. Which mix with sufficient powdered sugar and water to make a nice sherbet. Then add the remaining pistachios, and serve.

Almonds and fresh walnuts may be done the same way.

Çekirdeksiz Üzüm Hoşafı

SULTANI RAISIN HOSHAB

Ingredients

1 lb sultani raisins
1 pint of water
1 1/2 cup sugar
1-2 drops essence of orange-flower or rose

Take the stalks off sultani raisins and well wash them; put them in a stew pan with water, and set it to boil until they are swollen up.

Then take it off, and pass the liquor through a sieve into a saucepan, add sugar, and boil until it becomes thick, then remove it.

When cold, pour it in a glass bowl, and moderate the sweetness with cold water, then put the boiled raisins in, with a few drops of the essence of orange-flower or rose, and a few small pieces of ice, and serve.

All other raisins, currants, dried kinds of cherries, dried apricots, and dried plums of all kinds, may be done in the same way.

PART XIX.

ŞURUPLAR / SYRUPS

Şurup

PLAIN SYRUP

Ingredients

3 lb sugar
2 pint of water
1 egg
1-2 drops essence of orange-flower

Put sugar in a clean stew pan, with two pints of cold water, then whip up the white of the egg, and add it to the sugar. Stir well with a wooden spoon, and set it to boil until it becomes a little thick.

Skim it well, and, just before you take it off, add a few drops of the essence of orange-flower, or any other essence you choose, pass it through a clean cloth. When cold, bottle and cork it up until wanted.

Vişne Şurubu

CHERRY SYRUP

Ingredients

2 lb cherries
Sugar

Squeeze as the cherries, and pass the juice through a cloth into a basin, and leave it for twenty-four hours. Then strain it gently into another basin, and throw the residue away. Whatever quantity of juice is obtained put it in a very clean stew pan, with double the quantity of sugar; stir until the sugar is dissolved, and set it to boil.

As soon as it bubbles up take it off, and pass it through a sieve or cloth. When cold, bottle and cork it up until wanted.

Orange, pomegranates, currants, white, black, and red, are all done in the same way.

Vişne Şurubu II

MORELLA CHERRY SYRUP

Ingredients

1 lb cherries
3 lb sugar
2 pints water
1 egg

Put about sugar in a stew pan, with two pints of cold water, and the white of an egg, well beaten up.

Stir it well, and put it on the fire. When boiling, skim it well, and let it simmer until a little thick, then add the cherries with the stalks taken off, and well washed.

Let it boil gently for a few minutes longer, and then take it off. When nearly cold, take the cherries out with a strainer, and pass the syrup through a clean cloth, then bottle and cork it up. This will not be as acid and full-flavoured with fruit as the former one, but the colour is delicate and the drink is very agreeable. Red and black currants may be done in the same way.

Menekşe Şurubu

SYRUP MADE OF VIOLETS

Ingredients

1 lb violet leaves
2 pints water
3 lb sugar

Cut the stalks off the violet leaves, and put the them in a basin. Pour two pints of boiling water over, immediately cover it, and let it remain for twelve or fifteen hours. Then pass the liquor through a clean cloth into a stew pan, add sugar, stir with a wooden spoon until the sugar is dissolved, and set it on a charcoal fire.

Just as it commences to boil up, instantly remove, it, and let it remain covered till nearly cold. Then pass it again through a cloth, bottle and cork it up until wanted.

Sirkencebin

OXYMEL, or VINEGAR SYRUP

Ingredients

3/4 pint white wine vinegar
1 egg
3 lb sugar
1 small bunch sweet marjoram

Put in a saucepan the white of an egg, well beaten up, sugar, and pour in all at once white wine vinegar. Stir it once round with a wooden spoon, set it on a charcoal fire, and boil it for half a minute. Then skim and take it off, and instantly put sweet marjoram tied up in a piece of muslin, put the cover over the pan, and leave it until cold.

Then pass it through a clean cloth, bottle and cork it up until wanted. In summer days, it is an agreeable and refreshing beverage with cold water.

Ingredients

1 lb almonds
1tbls bitter almonds
1 1/2 pint of water
2 3/4 lb sugar

Badem Şurubu

ALMOND SYRUP

Scald the almonds, then skin and pound them in a stone mortar until in pulp. Mix it with half of the water, and pass it through a close muslin into a basin. Put the residue in the mortar and pound it again, which mix with the rest of the water, pass it again through the muslin into the basin. Then put in a stew pan the sugar, add the liquor, stir well with a wooden spoon, set it on a charcoal fire, and let it boil for one minute, then take it off, and pass it through the muslin again, bottle, and cork it up till wanted. It is a wholesome beverage.

Ingredients

3/4 pint lemon juice
3 lb sugar
1 egg
2 pints water

Limon Şurubu

LEMON SYRUP

Put sugar in a stew pan, with the white of an egg well beaten up, and two pints of water. Stir well and set it on the fire. When boiling, skim it well, and as soon as it begins to thicken add lemon-juice, and let it boil for half a minute longer, then take it off. When nearly cold, pass it through a clean, bottle, and cork it up till-wanted.

Ingredients

1 1/4 lb strawberries

Çilek Şurubu

STRAWBERRY SYRUP

Put sugar in a stew pan with water, and the white of an egg well beaten up, set it on the fire. When boiling, skim and simmer

3 lb sugar
2 pints water
1 egg

until it begins to thicken; then remove it, and immediately add fresh-gathered strawberries, well cleaned and the stalks taken off.

Put the cover over the pan and let it remain for two hours, then take out the strawberries with a strainer, and pass the syrup through a clean cloth; bottle and cork it up until required.

Demirhindi Şurubu
TAMARIND SYRUP

Ingredients

3/8 lb tamarinds
2 pint of water
3 lb sugar

Put tamarinds in an earthen pan with water, set it to boil until it is reduced to a pint and a half, then take it off and pass the liquor through a sieve into a stew pan. Add sugar, and boil it for half a minute, then take it off. When nearly cold, pass it through a clean cloth, bottle, and cork it up until wanted.

Gül Şurubu
ROSE SYRUP

Ingredients

1 3/8 lb roseleaves
1 1/2 pint of water
2 3/4 lb sugar
1 egg

Procure fresh gathered roseleaves. Pour in a very clean stew pan the water, put it on the fire. When boiling, put the rose-leaves in, and as soon as it boils up again take it off, put the cover over, and leave it until cold.

Then pass it though a sieve into the saucepan, and cast the residue away. Then add sugar and the white of an egg well beaten up, put the pan on the fire. When it boils up, skim and take it off, then pass it through a clean cloth, bottle, and cork it up till required. It is most pleasant syrup.

PART XX.

REÇELLER / JAMS

Çilek Reçeli / Strawberry Jelly

Vişne Reçeli
MORELLA CHERRY JAM

Ingredients

2 lb cherries
4 lb sugar
1 pint of water

Take off the stalks and extract the stones the cherries. Then put sugar in a stew pan with water and set it on the fire until it begins to thicken. Add the cherries, stir with a wooden spoon, and boil until rather thick.

Try a little on a plate, if it sets. Then take it off. When cold, fill the reserve jars, or glass bowls with covers, and let them remain in a cool place.

Apricots, greengages, quinces cut in pieces, green gooseberries, strawberries, raspberries, currants, red, black, and white, may all be done in the same way.

Ayva Murabbası
QUINCE JELLY

Ingredients

14 lb quinces
1 egg
3 lb sugar
6 pints water
2 lemon
1-2 drops of cochineal or red food colouring

Get quinces, peel them, cut each one in quarters, and remove the cores; then beat up the white of an egg in a stew pan, add sugar, and water, put it on the fire. When boiling, skim it; then add the fruit, and boil it until reduced to a pulp. Then take it off, and pass it through a clean cloth into another stew pan, add juice of the lemons, set it again on the fire, and let it boil gently for a minute or two. Then skim and pass it again through close muslin into the pan, add prepared cochineal, put it again on the fire, and let it boil until it becomes a thick syrup. Then take it off andfill the preserve jars or glass bowls. When cold, cover them, and keep them in a cool place.

Ayva Murabbası II
QUINCE JELLY II

Ingredients

3 lb quinces
3 lb sugar
4 quarts water

Peel and cut as above the quinces, put them in a stew pan with water, set the pan on the fire, and let it boil until the fruit becomes like a jelly. Then take it off and pass it through a cloth or a sieve into another pan. Add the sugar, set it to boil again till it becomes a thick syrup, then take it off, and strain it again.
When nearly cold, fill your preserve jars and cover them when cold; but, to be certain, try a little on a plate before potting. If it sets, it is done.

Gülbeşeker Şemsiyye
SUN COOKED ROSE PRESERVE

Ingredients

1 lb rose leaves
2 1/2 lb sugar

Cut the white ends of the roses with a pair of scissors and throw the white parts away. Put the rest in a basin with sugar and work it together with the hands until the rose leaves reduced to a pulp or a paste. Then fill the preserve jars or glass bowls and arrange them on a tray and put them under the sun. When near sunset put the cover over and take them in. The next day uncover the jars and expose the preserve to the sun as before, and continue the same for a month or until the top of the preserve is nicely crystallized It is a delicate confection and may be taken at breakfast or used with pastry.

Violet leaves may be done in the same way.

Menekşe Şerbeti

VIOLET SHERBET

Ingredients

1 lb violet leaves
5 lb sugar

Procure very fresh violet-leaves, put them on a convenient dish or a clean board, with sugar, and rub well together until the sugar becomes the same colour as the violet leaves. Then fill your preserve jars, cover them air tight, and put them by the sun. When wanted, especially in summer days, two or three teaspoons may be dissolved in a glass of cold water and be taken. It is a most pleasant and refreshing beverage.

Gülbeşeker

CONFECTION OF ROSE, or ROSE-JAM

Ingredients

1 lb rose leaves
3 1/2 lb sugar
3/4 pint of water

When the roses are in full bloom, gather the leaves, pick out the large ones, and cut the white ends off with a pair of scissors.

Then put the small ones and the white ends in a very clean stew pan with water, and scald them. Then pass the liquor through a piece of muslin or a sieve, squeeze well the leaves and throw them away. Put the liquor in the pan with sugar, and stir them with a wooden spoon till the sugar is dissolved. Then add the large leaves that you have picked out, stir and boil until rather thick. Try a little on a plate: if it gets, then remove it from the fire.

When cold, fill the preserve jars, cover them airtight, and keep them in a rather cool place.

DÖNENCE PUBLICATIONS

Sema Nilgün Erdoğan
SEXUAL LIFE IN OTTOMAN SOCIETY

Mehmet Gazali
BOOK OF SHEHZADE
A XVIth Century Ottoman Sex Classic

Anonimus
TURKISH ANECDOTES

Kemal Özdemir
OTTOMAN CLOCKS AND WATCHES

Kemal Özdemir
ORIENTAL BELLY DANCE

Cevat Ülkekul
JEAN GUERARD'S ATLAS OF AMERICA

The Ottoman Dishes seen on pages 20, 34, 40, 114, 131, 148 (buttom) and 152 were prepared by the Istanbul's finest Ottoman Cuisine restaurant,

ASİTANE

We wish to thank

ASİTANE

for permission to publish its photographs.